v

For You When I Am Gone

Twelve Essential Questions to Tell a Life Story

Steve Leder

AVERY
an imprint of Penguin Random House
New York

AVERY

An imprint of Penguin Random House LLC
penguinrandomhouse.com

Most Avery books are available at special quantity discounts for bulk purchase
for sales promotions, premiums, fund-raising, and educational needs. Special
books or book excerpts also can be created to fit specific needs. For details,
write SpecialMarkets@penguinrandomhouse.com.

Names: Leder, Steven Z., author.
Title: For you when I am gone: twelve essential questions to tell a life story /
    Steve Leder.
Description: New York: Avery, an imprint of Penguin Random House, 2022.
Identifiers: LCCN 2022004928 (print) | LCCN 2022004929 (ebook) |
ISBN 9780593421550 (hardcover) | ISBN 9780593421567 (epub)
Subjects: LCSH: Death—Psychological aspects. | Mourning customs. |
    Funeral rites and ceremonies.
Classification: LCC BF789.D4 L38 2022 (print) | LCC BF789.D4 (ebook) |
    DDC 155.9/37—dc23/eng/20220208
LC record available at https://lccn.loc.gov/2022004928
LC ebook record available at https://lccn.loc.gov/2022004929

Printed in the United States of America
1st Printing

Book design by Shannon Nicole Plunkett

To Aaron and Hannah,
our life and legacy

Contents

Introduction

No baby knows when the nipple is pulled from his mouth for
the last time. No child knows when he last calls his mother
"Mama." No small boy knows when the book has closed on the
last bedtime story that will ever be read to him. No boy knows
when the water drains from the last bath he will ever take with
his brother. . . . No mother knows she is hearing the word *Mama*
for the last time. No father knows when the book has closed
on the last bedtime story he will ever read.

—Jonathan Safran Foer

Consider the joke about a husband who thinks his wife is losing
her hearing. He gets so frustrated that he tells his doctor about
it. The doctor gives the man a test to try later in order to diag-
nose the severity of his wife's problem. "When you get home,"
the doctor advises, "stand about thirty feet away from your wife
when her back is turned to you and ask her what's for dinner. If
she doesn't hear you, move about fifteen feet behind her and ask
again. If she still doesn't hear you, stand just five feet behind her,
raise your voice, and say, 'What's for dinner?' That should tell
us how bad her hearing problem really is."

So the man goes home and asks his wife what's for dinner from thirty feet away. No answer. Fifteen feet away, again no answer. Finally, standing just five feet behind his wife, he shouts, "What's for dinner?" At which point his wife turns around and yells, "I told you three fucking times already, chicken!"

Sometimes, without even realizing it, we are deaf to the people around us and it's far from funny. This can be particularly true when it comes to children and parents. I remember when my son was sixteen and spent his summer as a counselor-in-training at a sleepaway camp in Malibu, California. After just two days he called me in near total frustration saying, "Dad, kids don't listen!"

"Thank goodness you and your sister were never like that," I replied. He got the point.

It's not just young children who sometimes miss the wisdom and the warnings of their loving parents. There is a chilling verse in a song by one of my favorite singer-songwriters, Steve Goodman. It's called "My Old Man." Goodman wrote it after his father, Bud Goodman, died. In this particular verse he sings about all the things his father said to him when he wasn't listening, and how much he wishes he could remember those things now that his father is gone.

A lot of people aren't aware of it, but there is a powerful and ancient way to speak to the people we love after we are gone so that they remember the most important things we said and taught them while we were alive. Jews have been doing it since the eleventh century in Germany, Italy, and Spain, and now virtually everywhere they live. Anyone can do it.

My own father was unaware of it, even before he lost his mind to Alzheimer's disease.

By a certain age, most of us have some sort of estate plan and a will to determine who inherits our material possessions and our money, if we are lucky enough to have extra when we die. Once that plan is complete and the will is signed, many people feel they have checked a box and done right by their heirs. We often forget about the other, more important treasures we have to give, the kinds of things I wish my father were still here to impart to me—our values, hopes, advice, deep love, and the accrued wisdom of a lifetime for those who will live on when we are gone.

I have been a rabbi for thirty-five years. In that time, I've presided over more than a thousand funerals, written more than a thousand eulogies, and sat with over a thousand families in the aftermath of losing loved ones. Being around death for so many years and the death of my own father have taught me that despite the fact we spend so much of our lives working to make money to buy things, collect things, wear and drive and live in things, those things matter little if at all to our loved ones when we are gone. Yes, our culture tries to teach us otherwise. We are raised to believe in the power of things and that our self-worth is somehow related to our net worth. If you doubt this, just try asking an acquaintance their net worth and see what happens. You have a better shot getting them to tell you whether or not they have hemorrhoids! Take a careful look at the ads in most magazines or most commercials on TV and you will see how we are seduced into granting real meaning to material things. Most advertising is not about the product itself but about the exciting or beautiful or meaningful life you will have by owning it. I will never forget seeing most of my father's "things" piled in a heap on the basement floor of my parents' townhouse after he died. No one wanted most of it, not even the thrift store. Abraham Joshua Heschel was right when he said, "To have more does not mean to be more." In other words, the purpose of life is not to have, but to be.

One Mother's Day the writer Donna Freitas described what she was longing for from her mother, who had died seventeen years earlier.

This June will mark the seventeenth anniversary of my mother's death. Seventeen whole years of not speaking to my mother or telling her anything at all. Seventeen whole years of not asking her questions, of not calling her up on the phone to drive her crazy about something or other, seventeen entire years without her pestering me about something else or other either. Seventeen whole years of wishing I could ask my mother advice about my life, my choices, about whether or not I should have a child, about how I might survive a divorce. Seventeen whole years of wanting to hear my mother say to me, that she'd love me no matter what I chose, what befell me, what mistakes I might have made.

The word for *word* in Hebrew and the word for *thing* in Hebrew are the same word (*davar*). To me, this is a very deep, spiritual point. Words have heft and weight; they are as concrete and material as any "thing" we will ever own or leave behind.

So let us leave words for those we love in order that we may journey with them long after we are gone, and let it not take imminent death for us to find those words and craft a more meaningful legacy. This book will give you the right questions to ask yourself to find the words that really matter.

Perhaps most of all, my message is "Don't wait." Because none of us ever really knows which conversation might be our last.

When I reached out to a group of friends to answer for themselves, for the sake of their loved ones, and for you the questions upon which this book is based, I thought I was asking a favor. They are busy people, and I was inviting them to wrestle with some of life's most important and difficult questions.

Among them are African American, Indian, Caucasian, and Hispanic men and women, as well as gentiles, Jews, Muslims, and Hindus. They are straight and gay, single and married, cisgender and transgender, some with children and some childless. Some have parents who survived the Holocaust, others' parents died when they were children; still others have endured the death of a young spouse, battled addiction, battled depression, lost and won, lost and won. Some have suffered the death of their reputation in a way the entire country knew about, some have been incarcerated or had a child in prison, more than a few have survived cancer, some are famous, others are not.

Despite my feeling that each of these people would be doing me a large favor by agreeing to peer into their hearts and souls to face such questions, without exception every one of them thanked me instead. It was as if I had done them the favor. Why? I think first because we each have a story and we really do want to tell our story; we want it to be known, at least by the people we love most. The Nobel Prize–winning author Isaac Bashevis Singer said, "The dead don't go anywhere. They're all here. Each man is a cemetery. An actual cemetery, in which lie all our grandmothers and grandfathers, the father and mother, the wife, the child. Everyone is here all the time." It's literally true, in the sense that we have within us the DNA of family that came before us. It is also metaphorically true in the sense that we carry the stories, the experiences, the wisdom, the failures, and the beauty of each of the lives on our family tree that came before our own. And not just of family, but of everyone we care about, everyone who has in some way touched our lives. Of course, this is only true if we know the stories. Only then can we learn from and live with the values and ideals, the rights and the wrongs those stories have to teach. We cannot learn from a story no one has ever told us. My friends thanked me partly, I think, because we all want to share our stories with the people we love, but we often fail to take the time or don't know how to begin.

Telling our stories is for others and for us. It is one way to push back against fatalism, the idea that we are not in control of our lives or, worse, that ultimately our lives don't matter. They do matter, especially to the people who love us, and we can determine much of our own story and change the narrative as we go. But those changes depend on asking ourselves the right questions, questions that remind us of what is really important and shed light on the consequential choices of our lives. Once, when I was panicking over the fear of having made a terrible mistake, a friend said to me, "I have given up all hope of a better past." We cannot change the past, but we can change the future by understanding our past. The questions we are going to ask in this book can lead to greater clarity about our values and our dreams, and whether or not we are actually living those values and dreams or merely professing to. Telling our stories is a way to share whatever meaning and joy we have found along the way, the depth of our love for others and for life itself. It is a way of saying not only that we the storyteller matter, but even more so the beloved listener. To share our story with someone is to say, you matter to me.

And if we do not tell our story, who will?

My friends thanked me for another very simple and very complex reason. We spend a good deal of our lives putting off telling our stories to our loved ones in the way this book proposes because we spend a good deal of our lives denying death. For much of our lives, most of us avoid thinking about our mortality as much as possible. We have to. We are young, we are invincible, we are ambitious, and we do not want to think that it all could someday be for naught; that we could someday be for naught. Our friends, our parents, often even our grandparents are alive and well, thriving, laughing, and loving. Who wants to think it will ever be otherwise unless we must? We also live in a culture that keeps death at arm's length whenever possible. Most people do not die at home. Wherever we die, we are often whisked away by a van and not seen by our loved ones until we have been prettified with makeup and suitable clothes. We say things like "Rest in peace," as if the dead are merely taking a long nap. We use euphemisms like "We lost Grandpa" or "She's moved on."

Deep down we know that we are all merely flesh and bone and blood, subject to decline or disaster in years to come or tomorrow. To answer the questions in this book is to face the fact of our fleeting days. We all avoid looking directly into the sun, but does that mean its light is not shining all around us each day? So too the shadow of death. I suspect each and every one of my friends thanked me because each of them felt unburdened after facing their mortality in this way. Their answers give their lives shape, meaning, and a promise of continuity for each of them and for their loved ones when they themselves will die. I think the relief and satisfaction of telling his stories is what prompted one friend to say after I thanked him, "I am the grateful one." My friends felt somehow more, not less, immortal by contemplating their deaths in a form that chronicled their deepest beliefs and dreams for others. I think you will too.

❧

Rabbi Jonathan Eybeschütz, who died in 1764, was famous not only among Jews but among Christians as well for his great learning. One Shabbat morning, the rabbi was walking to the synagogue when he encountered the burgomaster of Prague, a prince of the royal family. "Rabbi, where are you going at such an early hour?" asked the prince.

"Your Excellency," replied the rabbi, "I know not where I am going."

The noble thought the rabbi was being flippant, so he ordered him arrested for public disrespect to the authorities. As he was being marched away in irons, the rabbi said to the burgo-master, "Your Excellency, you now see that I did not know where I was bound, for I thought I was going to the synagogue, and I am instead evidently going to the gallows."

At this the prince smiled and released him.

"You see," continued the rabbi, "I thought I was on my way to the synagogue, then to the executioner, and now I am once again on my way to the synagogue. None of us ever really knows where we are going."

We do not like to think about it, but the truth is, none of us has forever and none of us ever really knows for certain when death will come to us as either a shocking surprise or a peaceful friend. As much as there is a time to deny death in order to aspire, there is also a time to acknowledge it in order to fully live and cherish each moment. There is a time to share the deepest truths of our lives for our loved ones to know and to hold even when, especially when, we are gone.

The tradition of leaving words for our loved ones in the form of what my tradition calls an ethical will goes back a very long way. Many people were surprised to learn this when I wrote about the practice in my last book, *The Beauty of What Remains: How Our Greatest Fear Becomes Our Greatest Gift.* Nearly every interviewer on every talk show, news program, and podcast asked me about ethical wills because they had never heard of this ancient tradition before. Many also asked me to read a section of my own ethical will that was published in that book. I have included it again in this book at the very end as one example of what it might look like when you put all of your answers to the questions together. I put mine in the form of a letter to my two children.

Some would argue that the tradition of ethical wills dates back to the time of the Bible in Genesis 49:1–33. A dying Jacob gathers his sons to his deathbed to offer them his blessing. Other biblical examples of ethical wills include Deuteronomy 32:46–47, where Moses instructs the Israelites to be a holy people and teach their children. In his book *Ethical Wills: Putting Your Values on Paper*, author Barry Baines notes that the New Testament also contains illustrations of verbal ethical wills. He points to John 15–17, a recounting of Jesus's parting advice and blessings to his followers, and Matthew 5, where Jesus blesses his disciples. The early rabbis urged fathers to communicate the teachings and values of their tradition orally to their sons. Later they were written as letters.

The oldest written ethical will still in existence is by Eleazar, the son of Isaac of Worms (about 1050). When he was near death, Eleazar became more aware of his mistakes as a father and decided to make up for them in his ethical will. For example, he said, "Think not of evil, for evil thinking leads to evil doing. . . . Purify thy body, the dwelling-place of thy soul. . . . Give of all thy food a portion to God. Let God's portion be the best, and give it to the poor." In his letter, he cites what his sons should do, from reciting the Shema, a Hebrew prayer, at the correct hour to keeping water at the bedside in order to wash their hands quickly in the morning when they got up. Eleazar's will is also a good example of the way in which a parent can be honest about his or her shortcomings in a form that will endear a child to them more, not less.

These written letters, originally from fathers to sons as far as we know from what has survived, have become known as ethical wills. In his book *Hebrew Ethical Wills*, published in 1926, Professor Israel Abrahams, a leading scholar born in London in 1858 who wrote an important book about Jews in the Middle Ages, might well have coined the term. He collected and studied ethical wills for many reasons, not the least of which was that they "are among the richest sources of information that we have with respect to attitudes of medieval and early modern Jewish parents toward their children."

There are chilling, more modern examples of ethical wills written during the Holocaust. Many ask for retribution. A member of the Jewish Underground in the Białystok ghetto named Zippora Birman called in her ethical will for "Vengeance, vengeance—with no mercy, with no sentimentality."

Some Holocaust-era ethical wills are more hopeful, like this from a mother's will, published in the ghetto newspaper *Warsaw-Kraków* in 1940 and signed only "Your Mother":

Knowing this, will your heart still be heavy, my child? Will you still say you cannot stand your fate? But you must, my child, for so were you commanded; it is your calling. This is your mission, your purpose on earth.

You must go to work alongside people of other nations . . . and you will teach them that they must come to a brotherhood of nations and to a union of all nations with God.

You may ask, "How does one speak to them?" This is how: "Thou shalt not murder; thou shalt not steal; thou shalt not covet; love thy neighbor as thyself. . . ." Do these things and through their merit, my child, you will be victorious.

Eight decades later, in his answer to one of my questions for this book, a friend lamented the absence of words passed down from that generation:

I hugely regret never having taken an oral history from my mother before she died at a young age. She came to this country as a teenager from Gomel, Belarus. I never recorded any of her memories. I know nothing about the family that was there—most of whom perished in the Shoah [the Holocaust]. Who was my grandfather? What was he like? Where are the cemeteries in which family members of previous generations are buried? Why did Mom travel through Manchuria, China, and Japan in order to reach the United States? My roots are now untraceable. That means that my grandchildren have family memories that go back only until 1915. I am insanely jealous of families that can trace ancestors back many centuries—some even to the expulsion from Spain. We are an ancient people; I am a bit of a *luftmensch*, floating above the unreachable facts.

There is no doubt that ancient and modern ethical wills teach us much about their respective eras and their values, but most important, they teach us about the enduring values that span the millennia and transcend any one religious tradition. As Abrahams notes, "What binds together the premodern and contemporary traditions of ethical wills may be certain enduring human values, for in the end, love and generosity of spirit appear to be of ultimate significance." An ethical will often ends with an ultimate value that guided its author in life with the hope that it will guide their heirs when the author is no longer alive. One of my favorite examples comes from long ago in an ethical will by Joel, son of Abraham Shemariah, an eighteenth-century Polish Jew who concluded with this: "For the main thing is peace, peace with the whole world."

Despite my feeling I was imposing on them, my friends were not only grateful but flattered when I asked them to be a part of the exercise that we will all engage in as this book unfolds. I think this is because at some level we do not really believe our stories are all that interesting or important, or perhaps we think that we have no right to impose our views and values on others. To which I say, what a poorer and less beautiful thing life would be without the stories and values of the people who loved us and whom we loved most to carry with us when they are gone. Just as important, our loved one's stories can inspire us to tell our own. I have been leading ethical-will writing workshops all over the country for fifteen years, and every time someone stands to read their version at the end of the session, there are tears, not of sadness but of love expressed.

An ethical will, or a "legacy letter," as it is sometimes called, is now a regular part of many estate-planning attorneys' recommendations to their clients, as well as part of hospice and palliative care protocols, intended to bring patients peace of mind. And it does.

In her *Huffington Post* article "My Dad Created an 'Ethical Will.' Here's What That Means and Why You May Want One Too," writer Carrie Friedman put it this way:

As part of his own legacy plan, [my dad] kept
Dictaphone tapes of his verbal letter to us, his three

kids, in the event something sudden and tragic happened to him. Over the decades, he updated the tapes whenever my siblings or I got a new job or spouse, had a baby, got a dog or lost one.

"Keep it current," he told us and his clients. "Everyone should know how loved they are."

He prepared for the worst, but we were not prepared for what happened to him. Parkinson's and dementia overtook his brain, and within a couple of years, at the age of just 72, he could barely speak or walk. My titan of a father, this man who believed in building on the foundations of the generations before, could not remember our names, let alone the names of our children.

Because of what he's taught my siblings and me, and because of what I've seen happen to him, my husband and I often update our ethical wills on our computers. . . . I tell my daughters what I want them to know after I'm gone. I offer practical advice: "Try not to let another person's insecurities shape your own behavior and beliefs." "Always approach dogs with your palm facing up to the sky, so the dog knows you come in peace. Approach some people like this as well." And I offer some opinions: "Someday, you will consider getting a tattoo. Fine. Just not on the face. Never on the face."

"Please don't spend your college funds on collagen." I try to be funny. I try not to imagine how old they will be when they read them. More than anything, I make sure to express my unconditional love for them. I express it out loud, too, like my dad did.

For thirty-five years I have been gathering with families to talk about their loved one after he or she has died. I need to hear the stories not only to prepare a eulogy, but to help each family realize that people die but love and legacy do not. I am often asked how I have managed to sit with so many families over so many years to hear about people I did not know and to try to then capture the essence of that person in a few pages. My answer is always the same: If you ask the right questions, everyone's life is hilarious, sad, adventurous, foolish, and wise; everyone's life is interesting. Everyone's life is a textbook about your own life. Hearing other people's stories has enriched my life, informed my life, and ennobled my life. I would not have wanted it any other way.

When I sat down to figure out which questions to include in this book, it took me about fifteen minutes to come up with the list. Fifteen minutes and thirty-five years. For at least as long as I have been a rabbi I have been wrestling with which questions really matter, wrestling with the answers myself, and sitting with grieving families as they answer these questions on behalf of a loved one who has died, to get at not just the facts of their life, but more important, the truths. These questions are deliberate and so is the order in which I ask them. They have helped countless families tell the deepest, most honest, and often beautiful truths by which their loved one lived. Sadly, families are frequently only able to guess at the answers because the person who has died never took the time to share their own answers to these questions in a way that was clear and lasting. This book invites you to answer the same questions, to generate the material from which you can create an ethical will so that the people you love will never have to guess which values, which words, or which blessings will remain as your legacy to them when you are gone.

I have devoted a chapter to each of these twelve questions. In each chapter, I tell you why I believe the question is worth asking. Then I offer examples of answers shared with me by the many people I invited to participate in this book. They all understood that their words would be shared with you too. I hope you will be as moved as I am by their answers and that they will inspire you to join them in wrestling with the questions. Your specifics will be your own, of course, but you may also find yourself tapping into the universals of love, kindness, family ties, and forgiveness, to name a few. At the end of each chapter, I put the question to you.

I have written an ethical will to my children twice, once when I was forty and one at fifty-nine, after my father died. He suffered with Alzheimer's for a decade. Throughout that time I tried to make the trip from Los Angeles to Minneapolis to visit him every few months. I watched my dad slowly diminish but had no idea which conversation with him might be our last. I never imagined that during one visit he could speak and understand and the next he would remain almost entirely silent for the rest of his life. He has been dead for four years and now my mother, too, is suffering from dementia. I have changed as a result of my father's death and my mother's memory loss; so have my advice, realizations, dreams, and understanding of my own very real and serious flaws. Like me, my ethical will is a work in progress, unfolding as my life unfolds and I lose the people I love. We are all like that. We are all made up of our stories; the stories of our wounds, hard-earned wisdom, laughter, joy, suffering, healing, failing, and loving. There is much for us to teach within our stories and much for our loved ones to learn and hold on to. And after all, our stories are made up of words. Words are the most real and important things we can leave behind when we are gone. Because, as Carrie Friedman's dad said, everyone should know how loved they are.

Let us begin . . .

CHAPTER 1

What Do You Regret?

Make the most of your regrets; never smother your sorrow,
but tend and cherish it till it comes to have a separate and
integral interest. To regret deeply is to live afresh.

—Henry David Thoreau

When Mark was dying, I pulled a chair up to his bedside. We made small talk for a few minutes about his hospice treatment, and about how his wife and the kids in their blended family seemed to be holding up. Then we went deep. Mark spoke to me about a handful of things he was rightfully proud of; next he tallied his regrets. Like most people's, his regrets were not so much about what he had done. People generally grow to forgive themselves for their mistakes. Some people don't consider anything that has ever happened to them or that they have ever done to be a mistake because they made the best decision they could at the time with the knowledge they had. My friend Caroline put it this way:

> The truth is that there is nothing I would have done differently. Yes, some things turned out badly, but I could only see what happened in hindsight. But if I put myself back into the person I was, within the circumstances I found myself at the time I made the decisions, I would not change them. At the time, they were the right ones, even if I sometimes ended up not liking the outcome. My advice: if you don't like the way something turned out, don't waste your energy regretting it. Learn from it.

And one of my friends, who happens to be the mayor of a major city, went so far as to say:

> I have always tried to take each mistake and cherish it. It's win-win: the more mistakes you make, the more gifts of learning you will have; the fewer mistakes you make, you might be getting wiser and more skilled. A lot of people are afraid of taking action—they want someone else to go first, to figure out what went wrong, to improve it, perfect it, and then they will adopt it. How boring!

Others who have no regrets are people with faith that every decision and circumstance is ultimately in God's hands. "I don't have anything I wished I would have done," my friend Amanda told me. Amanda's young husband died of Covid-19, leaving her and their six-month-old baby behind. Still, she said, "I like to believe that God has led my life and put me where I need to be always, led me where to go always."

But Caroline, Amanda, and the mayor are in the minority. Most of us have very real regrets about our lives and most of us are like Mark—our regrets are not about what we've done with our lives, but about what we haven't done. I find this to be true of the vast majority of dying people I speak with. There is a reason the sages said that when we die, we will be "called to account for all of the permissible pleasures in life we could have enjoyed but didn't."

One of the things I always loved about Mark was how easily he laughed and how his whole face lit up when he did. So I decided to remind him of a story he told at our men's group many years before. The evening's topic was "What holds us back?" When it was his turn Mark described a party that he had gone to in his early thirties during the beginning of his relationship with the woman who would eventually become his first wife. In those days, Mark shed the suit-and-tie corporate lawyer persona that was required of him during the week by riding a black-and-chrome motorcycle on the weekends for fun. When he arrived at the party Mark put his motorcycle helmet and black leather jacket on the couch. For some reason he could not recall all those years later when telling the story, why he had gone to the party alone. What he definitely remembered was that once the party was getting loud and a little crazy, a beautiful woman picked up his motorcycle helmet and black leather jacket off the couch and shouted, "Whose are these? I wanna go for a ride!" And Mark said . . . nothing. "I have wondered for fifty years," he told the rest of us in that men's group, "what my life would have been like if I had said, 'They're mine. Let's go.'"

The psychologist William Marston asked three thousand people this brief question: "What do you have to live for?" He found that 94 percent of his respondents were simply enduring the present while they waited for the future. They were waiting for something to happen—waiting for the right man or the right woman; waiting for children to grow up; waiting to pay off the mortgage; waiting for a vacation; waiting for retirement; waiting to get involved in the community; waiting to learn some new skill or hobby; waiting, waiting, waiting. Ninety-four percent of us waiting, while each new day passes us by.

Years ago, one of my congregation's high school youth group members returned to Los Angeles after a semester in a small South American village. "What was the biggest difference between there and here?" I asked. "People are happier there," she said without hesitation. "They have much less than most of us, but they're much happier. They sing and dance more. They celebrate more. Families eat together. People take care of each other when they're sick. They help neighbors who are in trouble." When was the last time most of us sang and danced? How often do we sit together as a whole family to eat, and celebrate, and tease, and hug like a family ought to? How many of us even know our neighbors, let alone reach out to them when they're in trouble? And what about ourselves? How many of us are waiting instead of living? Waiting to start reading more, to start watching TV less, to start exercising, to be more present, to spend more time with our children and our spouses, to be a better brother or sister, son or daughter, colleague or friend? How many of us are waiting to garden, or paint, or hike, or relax, or get involved with our community or a charity to help the ill, the planet, or the desperately poor, the frail, and the lost? Ninety-four percent of us are waiting to seize the opportunities all around us, and then, slowly or suddenly, it's too late to go for the ride.

One of the surprising things I learned very early on in asking questions about a person's life is not only that most people regret the things they didn't do a lot more than what they did, but that there are remarkable commonalities among those things, as reflected in the answers I'm sharing with you here. Almost all of us end up regretting the same few kinds of missed opportunities.

For so many of us, it is the chances we didn't take and the dreams we did not pursue because we were consumed by meeting other people's expectations. It is the way we chose to suffer alone for far too long before reaching out for help. And it is the precious moments we missed forever because we failed to show up for the moments and people that mattered most. In this chapter, I have organized the examples according to these common themes that people who answer this question come back to again and again. The regrets you are about to read will hopefully help you think about and share your own so that those you love most will have far fewer.

I regret waiting for others to agree with me before pursuing my dreams. I got over that! Avoid it . . . by facing your fears. I recommend lots of failing—it files off the rough edges of disappointment and allows you to learn and grow instead of being stuck.

My biggest regret is that I did not listen to my soul earlier in my life. I am embarrassed at the pain and sorrow that I brought to my loved ones because I was "stuck on me." I know that the only way to avoid this error is to not worry about what looks good and just do good. I pray that my daughter, nieces, nephews, and grandson will follow my example of my recovery and live their purpose with passion and love.

❧

Do I even have the right to complain that I had a rich variety of professional options? I chose one—and I guess that I achieved a measure of success. But still—looking back over some eight decades of life—I wonder what my world would be like if I had chosen not just the profession I now occupy, but if I had found a way to actively sample what was behind door two and maybe even door three? Over the years, I was presented with an opportunity to head an international body dealing with intra- and interfaith relations. I was also offered an opportunity to earn a doctorate and to enter academia in a field of study that I adore.

I chose door one. And I operated with the widely held assumption that a profession once chosen must be lived throughout one's working days. With our longer life span today, with the proliferation of second or even third careers, I could have enriched my life by being open to change. Who would I be if I had been open to the kind of growth that change and innovation might bring? Could I have found newer and better ways to heal the world, to protect and preserve my people, to push back against the relentless tides of tribal hatred? I'll never know.

But what I do know is that I encourage my grandchildren to be more open than I was to discovering that there are multiple paths to fulfillment.

A day-to-day regret, and one that is entirely treatable, is allowing others around me to define my self-worth. Many times, the observations of others say more about the critic than the object of criticism. I believe that we are all hard-wired to jealousy, and there is no reason to be naïve about it. Jealousy is the source of the evil eye; the challenge is to turn away from that eye in order to see the landscape.

My biggest regret is making decisions out of fear and insecurity and not believing enough in myself to make critical decisions from a place of confidence and faith. Because of my upbringing, I didn't have that nurtured sense of self and felt very insecure about who I was and where I came from and at times did not have enough confidence in my talent and instincts to believe I belonged. Others had gone to Ivy League schools, had famous parents, lots of money, and I had none of those things. For a significant part of my young career, I truly felt insufficient and less worthy than others I was competing with. At a critical crossroads in my career, I chose the path of least resistance, thinking it was probably better to go the lighter route. It was the wrong decision and would cost me greatly. It caused a detour that took years to recover from, but it taught me such a valuable lesson. I had forgotten that what got me to the highest echelons of my business was my own experience and lens on the world and, yes, my gifts and talents as a writer and storyteller. In comparing myself to others, I diminished the gifts I had to offer and made decisions critical to my future based on a false sense of my weaknesses. It took me years to find my way back, but I value that which I do possess and have to offer and now tell my daughter to have confidence in who she is and what she brings to the world and to make decisions not based on fear or insecurities but on her greatest desires and highest potential.

If I had to pick one, I think I'd say I regret my inability to put my own needs first sometimes. It is possible to say no with grace. It is possible to let go of what other people think of you sometimes. It is possible to worry about others' needs without only worrying about others' needs. And it's terribly unfair to resent others when you've chosen not to prioritize yourself.

❧

I spent too much time comparing, judging, seeking approval, being hurt, wanting approval, looking outward for happiness. Now I want to forgive, to accept people for who and how they are. I can't waste time trying to change them, I can only change my expectations of them. I don't want to spend time anymore being hurt. If someone "disrespects me"—Big Freakin' Deal! It doesn't matter. Maybe their soul is undeveloped and they just don't know better. At this stage in my life, I want to MOVE ON—and clear out any ugliness in my heart.

❧

My parents had no money but, looking back, they gave me everything that was important: love, my drive, great values, and they saved everything they could to provide me an exceptional education. Considering everything they gave me, I wanted to be a success, not just for me, but also for them. I had to prove their sacrifices were worth it.

At the age of thirteen I knew I would be a lawyer and planned to get through college in two years. School was a job. Fun was not the goal. Doing something I might be passionate about was not an option. I loved economics, but what would getting a Ph.D. and potentially teaching at a mediocre college really prove, other than I could be just a struggling professor?

Not only did I not pursue what I was passionate about, but I didn't take advantage of the college experience, because that could get in the way of my future. My focus was on getting a law degree from a top law school and getting a great job. I had no idea what being a lawyer meant or required, but I did know it could be financially rewarding.

As luck would have it, I am passionate about my work. I love my job. But I regret giving up the joy of those ten years when you evolve from a kid to an adult. For that sacrifice I am sad and have regrets. It would be just as significant to say I have practiced law for thirty-nine years instead of forty-one, and had fun during four years of college.

The lesson for my children: I have tried to teach my kids that growing up is one chapter of their lives that they need to enjoy. Don't be me.

～

My biggest regret is not asking for help early enough. It took me a long time to realize that asking for help was not a weakness but a sign of confidence, character, and generosity. By asking for help, I have built deeper, more honest relationships. I have overcome challenges with people by my side, and we have celebrated together. I want my loved ones to know the sense of connection and empowerment from asking others for help.

～

I wish I had gotten better therapy earlier (both talk therapy and psychopharmacological); and I wish my wife and daughter would too. It has made a great difference in my life, and it would have made a great difference earlier if I had done so.

～

I regret that for the first nearly thirty years of my life, I was afraid of letting on that I didn't know everything. I feared allowing anyone to see me as weak. I was embarrassed by the awkwardness of learning new things, and that made it very hard to ask for help when I needed it, and it prevented me from pursuing some paths. I'm glad these views finally became untenable and I learned how to screw up and still love myself.

Slow down and enjoy the day. Be present. I wish I had savored each moment rather than being in the moment thinking about what I needed to do next. Specifically, I wish I had taken more trips, even visited local things, particularly with my husband, because there is no better way to make memories than to have experiences, especially travel, together.

My biggest regrets all center around time. I didn't take enough time to appreciate what was happening in the moment sometimes and just kept pushing through, which served the mission and my purpose, yet I realize the things I missed. I regret not spending more time in the awareness of wonder and radical amazement in my life and in the world. I regret that I didn't always see my responsibility in what was going on around me.

The one regret I carry most is having blazed through the moments that matter, not being present and missing so much connection and true intimacy that is only possible when we are truly focused in the moment. I have traveled to so many places and yet know only hotel rooms and venues, as work took precedence over really exploring the places I have been. I have met and worked with so many interesting people but have been focused on the work at hand and missed opportunities for real exchange and experience.

This may sound crazy but feeling joy doesn't come naturally to me. Working does. I've been so focused on getting things done, being successful, meeting that goal, completing that project as if playing a part in a movie but not really living the joy of it all. I tended to bypass experiences—the memories that deep-dive into the marrow of the moment—in order to drive forward and complete some agenda, and I regret that. I think there is a fear in that kind of abandonment. Truly being present with others and not hiding behind some shield of work or reason for being there requires confidence that your presence is enough.

At my daughter's bat mitzvah, I told her to say yes to life. That was my greatest hope for her. I long to infuse in her the power of holding another's gaze, putting your face to the wind and fully feeling the cool breeze and mist kiss your skin, opening your heart to nature and feeling the transformative power of truly letting go. I long for her to laugh out loud with abandon, to feel free to be exactly who she is and know that is enough and that it's okay to share her insides with the outside world, to fully capture and drink in the glorious moments no matter how small.

~

I don't have many regrets; this comes naturally to me—living in the moment. When I was fifteen years old my dad died suddenly in a plane crash, and not having regrets really helped me get through a crisis.

If anything, I like to impress upon my loved ones the importance of living in the moment, trying your hardest to do your best to make sure you don't have any regrets because you really don't know what tomorrow will bring. Try to live like every day is a gift, which I believe is true.

I regret wasting time fretting, worrying, spending time trying to make things be a certain way. My grandmother apparently had a saying: "I don't worry about the things I can't control." I wish I had been able to spend more of my time in that headspace.

There was the time I left the music festival at 2:30 a.m. deciding I wasn't going to wait for Jimi Hendrix to show up because I figured I'd see him some other time. Three weeks later he was dead. So I suppose the lesson is: Don't delay and have patience. And don't let an opportunity pass you by.

Mamma died alone in that crappy little hospital room in Newton, Mississippi. She should have died with all of us with her, holding her as she held us for all of our lives. We should have been there to soothe her the way she soothed us, we should have been there to comfort her as she made her journey out of this life. My entire adult life, Mamma would stand outside of her home when my sister and I would leave her to go back to our lives. She would stand at the end of the gate and wave to us until we couldn't see her anymore. We should have been there to witness her departure from this life.

If I have any regret, it's that I wish I had done an even better job of teaching our kids how important sticking together and looking out for each other really is. I thought I did a good job—talked a lot about it—but while I know they all love each other and would definitely be there in a crisis, they don't seem to be too interested in keeping up with each other as often as I would like and I am not sure they make each other feel loved all the time.

I wish I knew the answer to avoiding this. I hold out hope that maybe this is just a phase and as they get older, they'll realize how important siblings are to one another. I say never lose hope.

Among my top five regrets is missing a sixtieth anniversary party for my parents because of a speaking engagement. The latter was a minor event in my life; missing my parents' last big party continues to come up in therapy, usually with my tormenting myself until I again find the resolution to "just show up" and not risk another regret.

Having aging parents should have made my choice obvious. These decisions are not always obvious. Sometimes one intends to go, but there seems to be plenty of time to procrastinate. A bigger regret was my not showing up to see my grandson in his new preschool, his first foray into the social world after years of his grandmother's love and home care. Grandparents were allowed to visit any school day. It was far and I knew I'd get there one convenient day in spring or summer. Tragically, Jeremiah drowned during the July 4th weekend. I would give a fortune to spend just one day watching him play.

So, a critical message of my ethical will is having the humility and wisdom to admit we never know how much time we or our loved ones will have on earth. Act as if there may be no second chance—because there may not be—and don't risk the heartbreaking regret of not showing up.

❧

I regret not spending more time with family and friends. I regret the actions that I took that were seen to be off-putting and people dropping me. I regret not being more responsible earlier in my life and being in prison instead of raising my daughter. I regret that I didn't make enough trips to the East Coast to spend time with siblings, nieces and nephews, extended family, my mother. I regret being "too busy" at too many times.

❧

I am part of a big family, but I have never married and have no children. I don't even have a dog. While I do not believe that marriage and family are necessarily for everyone, I often wonder how my life might have been enhanced by the joy of having a wife and kids. Did I miss out on the real meaning of life? I wish I had made a greater effort to communicate directly with my siblings more often. As one of ten children, it's not always easy to stay in touch with all nine siblings. Our mother is usually the point of contact. As such, we are not as close as we were growing up. So, I wish I had reached out to spread love more often, especially as the big brother.

❧

I wish that I had reached out to others more often in both large and small ways. When I was younger, I was so shy and self-conscious that I would literally freeze. It took me decades to get over my paralysis. I am sorry I missed out all those years. I wish I had been more helpful.

❧

My biggest regret is all the time I have spent somewhere else while I'm physically in the presence of my loved ones. Thinking about how to solve some problem somewhere else, as worthy as that cause may be, has come at the cost of my full attention with the people I cherish. It's not simply a function of putting down the phone. Breathing intentionally in each moment and holding the present always teaches me something. It helps me feel more deeply, sometimes pain and grief as well as love. But when I do so, I understand more and can really be there for my people.

❧

Fear has held me back from doing things I wanted to do. My hope is that my loved ones overcome the fear of following their intuition and purpose.

I regret waiting too long to intervene with a friend who was suffering because I was scared that she would cut me out of her life. Perhaps I could have alleviated some pain, and I will always question my timing. Ultimately, I did an intervention, and it was as hard as

I imagined. She cut me out of her life for two years. But after a deep healing process, she is in a better place and I have no regrets about my ultimate decision. We are now closer than ever.

~

When our children were young, I spent a lot of time building my medical practice. As a result, I missed part of their upbringing. My wife did a great job with them, however. I know they love me and I love them as well. But I will never know all that I missed.

Now it's your turn.

What is your biggest regret and how can your loved ones avoid the same? What do you wish you had done, why, and what will doing that thing hopefully bring to your loved ones' lives that you missed out on?

Do you have regrets like the ones you have just read? I know I do, and I know that over the past three and a half decades of listening to others' regrets, I have learned much that has helped me avoid some of those same regrets, granting me a less painful, more beautiful, and more meaningful life. I hope sharing my remaining regrets will help my children in that same way.

We start with this question for a reason. Beginning with regret demonstrates fearlessness and truth-telling. It shows vulnerability and honest reflection that add credibility and depth to our answers to all of the questions that follow. Most of all, beginning by honestly acknowledging what we did not do but wish we had may well enable our loved ones to avoid, at least a little more than they otherwise would have, living to meet others' expectations at the expense of their own dreams, the fear that keeps so many of us from reaching out for help, and missing opportunities to celebrate life and share more love, not only at important moments but every day. Speak openly of your regrets with truth and vulnerability so that your loved ones learn from you now and when you are gone.

CHAPTER 2

When Was a Time You Led with Your Heart?

Your vision will become clear only when you can look into your own heart. Who looks outside, dreams; who looks inside, awakes.

—Carl Jung

I do not come from a family of risk takers. All four of my siblings live within a few miles of the Minnesota home in which we were raised. The 1960s suburb I grew up in was a place of conformity, where the appropriate posture was always one of bowed humility and social convention; the ideal was to stay one step behind the Joneses. My father often dismissed creativity as frivolous. Plain was always better than fancy when it came to virtually all people, places, and things. My three sisters all went to the same university because Dad insisted they attend college somewhere no more than a day's drive from home with all-female dorms and a curfew, and if it was good enough for one, it was good enough for three in his mind, and theirs.

Worst of all, there was always an impending sense of doom during my childhood, generated by my dad. He grew up poor, burning-wax-paper-in-the-Minnesota-winter-to-stay-warm-at-home poor. He had only two pairs of pants in his teens, one for work, which he washed each night, and the other pair for everything else. When I was young my father buried gold coins in the false bottom of a cabinet in the basement and under an oak tree in the backyard in case, as he put it to me, "God forbid we should ever have to run away and need to buy bread." I was just a little boy, now frightened by the prospect of becoming destitute or having to make a run for it from some amorphous, Nazi-like oppressor. One of the expressions he often quoted, translated from the Yiddish, was, "Even a cat can fuck it up." It was his way of saying that every move, every decision, every angle, every potential threat has to be carefully and thoroughly considered because some small, unanticipated thing could come along and cause a disaster. If you didn't use your head, you could metaphorically or literally end up dead. It was a frightening way to grow up and is behind much of the anxiety I sometimes suffer from so painfully today, anxiety that can suck the fun out of life for days, weeks, even months.

Despite this fearful and anxious upbringing, there were two times in my life that I nevertheless led with my heart rather than my head. Each put me at odds with my father. The first was when I decided against going into the family scrap metal recycling business or to law school and chose rabbinical school instead. When I told my father that I had decided to apply to the seminary after finishing college, his response was, "Rabbis are beggars." It was his way of cautioning me against working for anyone other than myself and very likely came from his own experience of having been asked for money time and time again by his own rabbis through the years.

My dad was right, but only in the small ways. Yes, to be a rabbi is to serve thousands and not to be entirely in control of your own career path, to be subject to a board of trustees, criticism, and the expectations others foist upon you because of their own sometimes weird relationship with your role. There are funerals, so many funerals, so much sadness, disease, divorce, despair, and dysfunction that I have to help others through, often at the expense of my own family and soul. And yes, there is the begging. There is truth in the old wisecrack that says, "It used to be that the wealthy lined up at the doors of the wise. Now the wise line up at the doors of the wealthy." I am ultimately responsible for the welfare of a massive institution that requires tens of millions of dollars a year to accomplish its mission, and it's often my job to find that money. That "begging," as my father put it, is stressful, sometimes demeaning, always exhausting, and it is never enough.

And yet I knew from the time I was a young boy that I was born, called, shaped, and formed for the rabbinate. The wonder the Bible stories held for me, the quiet grandeur of my childhood sanctuary, the soulful creativity in the music and the poetry in the ancient tongue, the learned rabbis, the comfort I felt only among my own, and the sense of transcendent meaning that defines all spiritual pursuits spoke to my heart. Difficult as it has often been, I cannot imagine having ever done anything else that would have felt as meaningful to me.

Not long after I told my father about my decision, I remember my college girlfriend's father saying to me, "I would be so proud if my son decided to become a rabbi." It might not seem like much now, but in that moment I realized that not every father feared any decision not made out of fear that a cat was somehow going to fuck everything up; that there were people who were proud when their children led with their hearts, and I could be proud I was leading with mine.

For many years after my ordination, when I was delivering a sermon on the pulpit, my parents would leave early in the morning from Palm Springs, where they wintered, and drive to Los Angeles to hear me preach. No matter how many people attended the service, when I looked out at the congregation the widest smiles of all were my mom's and dad's.

That decision to become a rabbi not only changed my life, it made my life.

The second time I led with my heart was a decision over which I felt I had no control and no other choice. A truth self-evident in a way unlike any other I have ever known. Many people have been fortunate to feel that same truth at least once in their lives.

I remember it as if it had happened today: Cincinnati, Ohio, February of 1984. I am in my office at the part-time job I held during rabbinical school running the Sunday school for a small synagogue. In walks the art teacher with a friend. "This is Betsy, she's visiting with me today," she says. I am overwhelmed and the only thing I hear is "This." Meeting Betsy's blue eyes and shy gaze, my soul wakes up. (I never understood the expression "The eyes are the window to the soul" until that moment.) I am in love. Later I would learn that Betsy felt exactly the same.

We agreed to have dinner together that evening. Dinner turned into a twelve-hour date, mostly sitting by the Ohio River talking effortlessly about our lives. My recent breakup, her recent battle with cancer, her failed relationship waiting for her back in New York City, our dreams and likes and loves, our families, our pain . . . Cut to our next date. We are sitting on the couch in my apartment ready to leave for dinner and a concert. I feel compelled in a way unlike ever before to speak from my heart. "Betsy, I think you're it."

"I feel the same way about you," she answered.

"So, are we engaged?" I asked.

"I guess so," she said in a way that felt like we had both merely affirmed the existence of the most obvious thing in the world, like gravity or oxygen.

Then, at twenty-four years old, having known her for only a few hours, I called my parents to tell them I was getting married. "To who?" was their shell-shocked response.

"To this girl I met last week," I answered, without any sense of how frightening that must have sounded to them.

My dad spoke first. My father was a guy who had great intuition, street smarts, and clarity about his own beliefs. He famously once said to my younger brother, "I thought I was wrong once, but I was wrong."

"Steven, you are not getting married," he snapped. "You are thinking about getting engaged."

Now I was the certain one and so I shot back in a tone and with language I had never before used with my father, "Dad, don't fuck this up. I am getting married."

To which my mother, who always understood matters of the heart better than he, simply said, "We look forward to meeting her."

The result of this decision made entirely from the heart has been nearly four decades of laughter, love, children, sometimes too little money, sex and no sex, my battle with anxiety, with spinal injury and surgery and the opioids and depression that followed, hers with six surgeries from a new cancer and another disease, kids in trouble, kids making us so proud, more laughter, family and friends who love us, others who let us down, seeing the world together and then learning to love just being home, wordless but so content holding hands beneath the covers. We wound, we heal, we offend, we forgive, we ache, we worry, and we carry each other through it all, come what may. We count our blessings and thank God we have each other.

When you ask nearly every person what matters most to them, they answer that it's their family, their work, or some passion to which they have devoted much of their life. Ask those same people how and why they chose to devote their lives to those people, professions, or causes, and they will almost always tell you it was the result of listening to their heart rather than taking the more conventional, rational path, the choice expected by others. This is one of life's most powerful lessons. Don't just take it from me. Listen to those I asked.

～

I have to ask myself, what is heart and what is head? I believe listening to God is listening to my heart.

On January 22, 2019, I finally surrendered, and told the truth to Bob and the doctors, the truth about myself, that I had fallen back into drug addiction. I was coming out of a grand mal seizure caused by an overdose of pain medication that I had been getting from China and India, clueless as to what was in them.

Finally, I had that sliver of willingness, that touch of grace, to come clean about my relapse. I had been to the emergency room many times before due to overdoses, but for some reason, God/grace/my heart was able to break through my denial in that moment and led me to be completely honest and surrender. It saved my life.

~

What brought me to join the anti–Vietnam War protest at the Washington Monument? Certainly not my head! I was an army chaplain. I so despised the war being prosecuted by young men and women who were wearing the same uniform that I was that I did not see that I had a choice. So I sang, I shouted, I applauded, I waved my fist, and I proclaimed my willingness to keep on fighting for what I considered to be justice and morality. All the while I had on my army uniform festooned with captain's bars. (After basic training, the only clothing that fit me was my army uniform.) The next day, I had the kind of meeting with the post commanding general that no captain would ever look forward to. But the war was wrong. I went to where I had to be.

Martin Luther King's assassination initiated a brutal tectonic shift in American society. What kind of a world do we live in? I knew what I would be choosing to do in the months that followed. But that night? The night of King's death? It was not intelligence that propelled me into Bronzeville, the historic epicenter of the African American community in Milwaukee, that night. The city was under lockdown; Chicago was burning. People were in the streets, howling their outrage. There were Black ministers and community leaders who had become not just colleagues but friends and partners. I could have stayed in my secure suburban home that night. That would have been rational. But my heart was bleeding. I drove into midtown. We hugged. We wept. And we began to plan.

Self-preservation is rational. My wife told my kids as I flew off to Moscow to be prepared that they might not see me again for quite a while. I was part of a small group in New England that wanted trained rabbis to enter Soviet Russia to bring religious supplies and other desperately needed items to the families of Jewish refuseniks who had lost their positions in academia and in the world of commerce because they were insisting upon their rights to leave the USSR for Israel or for the United States. I had been protesting and marching and organizing for the release of my brothers and sisters. I had been arrested outside of a Soviet consulate. I had traveled to Brussels to the first world conference on Soviet Jewry. But now I decided—literally—to put my freedom if not my life on the line. I smuggled in large amounts of contraband. I taught in an underground Jewish nursery school. I went from apartment to apartment with a message of hope. My hotel room was bugged. I was constantly followed. My people were crying, "Let us go." I helped.

My children know these stories—and their own lives reflect that awareness. I am trying to explain what obligations I feel as a human being and as a Jew for the well-being of my people and for all others. The decisions that I made not only were driven by the meditations of my heart, but by my hope that future generations will accept my acts as a template for the decisions that they will be called upon to make for themselves.

❧

I came out as a gay man in my mid-thirties. I finally realized that I had to live as who I really was and not pretend to be someone I was not. My heart had always told me who I was, but my brain convinced me to try and be someone I was not. Once I dealt with my sexuality, my life was never the same. I became a much more authentic person, more compassionate, and I relieved myself of a lot of anger. Ever since then I have been blessed with an overall wonderful life.

I love this question because leading with my heart has always brought my greatest blessings. There have been many that I could share—the time I turned down the bigger-paying job for the one that felt right in my heart that led to bigger positions in the end. But if I had to pick the greatest of them all, it would be the decision to adopt my beautiful little girl when I was in my late forties. There were many voices dissuading me from doing this in this late stage of my life, with an older husband at the time and me struggling to find my footing in my career. It was not the ideal time and there were many pressures that my brain clearly zeroed in on, all the reasons why this was not a reasonable nor intelligent thing to do. I had worked all my life; creating a family was never a priority for me until I got married late in life and for the first time felt a deep inner longing to be a mother and have a daughter. It was a decision that came purely from my heart, and despite fear, my age, my tenuous financial situation, I adopted this precious being from Guatemala and brought her home to America and it is the greatest decision I have ever made. So many have remarked what a wonderful gift I have given this child. The truth is, she is my greatest gift, my teacher, my greatest love, my deepest prayer.

⬧

In summer 1993, I decided to go on a trip to the mountains of Colorado, specifically to follow my heart—with no agenda. I aimed to drive into the mountains, wake up every day with a fresh start, and follow whatever road my intuition inspired. Within a few days I landed in Taos, New Mexico, where I met Phillip, who jumped onto my spontaneous adventure, and we spent a few days hiking in the mountains and soaking in hot springs by the Rio Grande, fishing with his six-year-old son, Alex, just going with the flow. I made it back to New York after that trip, but despite every logical reason that it was a totally insane thing to do, six months later I moved to Taos to form a family with Phillip and Alex. Twenty-eight years later and I'm still married, mother to Alex (and two others), and none of it would have happened if I'd followed my brain instead of my heart.

I believe I have led with my heart more often than not. I left the law and decided to write a book about a trial in Israel, based on my heart. That set me on my life's path. I've consistently danced to the beat of my own drummer.

I suppose if I had followed my head, I would have made a better living, but by following my heart I've had a much richer life—actually an amazingly full and interesting life. The people I've met, the places I've been, the experiences I've had—all quite remarkable and beyond my own expectations or imagining.

When I met my husband, our families lived on opposite sides of the world. Our relationship was completely impractical from a logistics point of view. But my heart had complete clarity and I knew he was my life partner. We decided to get married within two weeks of our first meeting, were formally engaged in four months, and a year later had a week-long wedding with thousands of people. We are celebrating our twenty-fifth wedding anniversary this year, have two amazing daughters and a loving extended family. I can't wait for our fiftieth.

Apology and forgiveness are a perennial lesson, and a lesson of the heart, not the head. When you offend or otherwise mess up, get out of your head and muster the courage to lead with your heart. Offer a sincere apology, make no excuses, and endeavor to not make that particular mistake ever again. Conversely, be willing to forgive so you can live. Let go of grudges. They destroy families and ruin relationships.

When I was eighteen years old, I ran after a handsome twenty-year-old boy and blocked him from entering the restroom at a restaurant we were both dining at. I knew him—he wasn't a stranger. In fact, I had dated his brother. I was nervous but followed him, and said to him, "When you get rid of her"—he had a girlfriend at the time—"and you will . . . give me a call." Then I ran back to my table. A year and a half later, a friend of mine bumped into the boy, knew how I felt about him, and encouraged (pressured) him to call me. He did. Thirty-seven incredible years, three wonderful children, and nearly four decades of joy, laughter, tears, and adventure later, the rest is history.

This is almost too easy because I cannot remember many times I led with my heart and not my brain. I used to think I was like Spock on *Star Trek*. All about logic. Marrying my wife was the one time I can say I led with my heart and not my brain.

Intellectually she checked all the boxes for me: she was beautiful inside and outside, kind, outgoing, and considerate of others. Everyone loved her. A friend who is a brutal judge of character said the first time she met her that I would be an idiot not to marry her.

All sounded logical, but she didn't check the Jewish box. For years that had been the death knell to my marrying someone. My parents were Holocaust survivors and I had the weight of the Jewish people on my shoulders. How could I let my parents down? How could I let my people down? Frankly, how could I let myself down? But in my heart and gut I knew she had the most important Jewish trait: great values. Frankly, she is the perfect Jew.

I led with my heart, which obviously turned out to be the best decision of my life.

I didn't want to have a third child. My husband, who came from a family of three children, kept asking me, but I was afraid of the sleeplessness, all the extra work, and the lack of "me" time. I said no for eight years; two children were enough. One day, when I picked up my older kids from school (ages eleven and eight at the time) and they chatted endlessly about what they had learned in class and I saw their little faces and dirty hands from their day, I was filled with such love. I had been concentrating on the hard parts of being a parent and had forgotten about the joy. In other words, I was too logical and not emotional enough. I went home and told my husband, "Let's try for a third." And we were lucky.

When I graduated college, I followed my college boyfriend to Los Angeles. I did not have a job lined up. I didn't have my own apartment. My parents were very concerned and didn't hesitate to let me know. But I was in love, and I had a feeling about him and our relationship. Honestly, I know he was not as certain as I was, but I looked past that, and decided I could be certain enough for us both. In hindsight, clearly, it was a big risk. We were very young, and while he was about to start law school in LA, and had his entire family in town, I was pinning everything on choosing him. Today, we're about to celebrate our twenty-fourth wedding anniversary. Even though I generally do believe it's important to use your heart and brain in concert, sometimes letting your heart be the guide can pay off, as long as you understand the risks and are nimble enough to reorient yourself if need be.

~

I have led with my heart/soul for most of my recovery and, truth be told, even before then. Leading with my soul leads me to joy, wonder, love, truth, kindness, compassion, and justice. I am able to know the next right thing to do, and when I follow my soul's knowledge, I live compatible with God. I love life and life loves me, whether I get what I hope for or not. Living from my soul brings me to clarity, acceptance, and living the principles I believe in.

~

After the shooting at the Tree of Life Synagogue in Pittsburgh, I remember standing before a sea of faces at the Federal Building alongside people of different faiths to mourn and grieve with one another. I felt so angry that this could happen. The story was unfolding that the perpetrator was angry at Jews for bringing in Muslim refugees to America. I knew I needed to be there, to show up for friends who have shown up for me at my own mosque when the threats rolled in years before. Doing so meant I would go against the policy of my organization to not make statements. I pushed forward anyway. Knowing that I needed to show up. It meant going against a calculated decision by many people I respect, but my heart said otherwise. So I worked as fast as I could to inform and consult them. I thought it would be an uphill climb, based on past experiences, but this time, their hearts understood too.

That day, my heart led the way. It held pain and grief with everyone else at the Federal Building. I was precisely where I needed to be. Since then, I have always consulted my heart. Prior to that moment, I had leaned on my mind to navigate life and undervalued the direction my heart pointed to. Had I listened to my brain, I likely would have stayed home out of fear and protectionism. There are risks in leading with the heart and yet I now can't see living any other way.

Insanely, ten days after our twenty-year-old cat died, I insisted on adopting a new one. She had been rescued from the To Be Destroyed list at Animal Care and Control. She'd been abandoned at least twice. She had an underlying medical condition that made her difficult to care for, and she had been labeled "vicious." Our vet was very skeptical of the decision. But I had seen her photo, and I knew that she was our cat.

She turned out to be the sweetest, most affectionate animal of any kind I have ever known. She was zen about life, a good sport about taking her special food and medications, and an unfailingly loving companion from the day she walked in and refused to leave us, even to explore the other rooms. When she finally died nine years later, of something entirely unexpected, we were devastated. But we also knew that we had won.

At the end of Eddie's life, I led with my heart and compassion for him. I didn't want to lose my husband, my children's father, but he was suffering and it was time to let him be at peace. It obviously changed my life forever in terms of him not being here, but it also made me realize how much I missed the physical presence of him, even if he required my care. I tell people often to hug the ones they love and always, at the end of life, to touch their hand, kiss them, because once that is gone it will be missed.

⁓

When was a time you led with your heart rather than your head? Why and how did that change your life?

A psychiatrist once told me that the reason children and adolescents do foolish things is that their brains are not fully developed. Lacking the necessary part of the brain for considering the potential consequences of their choices, they mostly consider only the reward. As we mature, we factor in the potential downside of nearly all of our decisions. We become more risk averse and less spontaneous. How ironic then that for most of us the people and pursuits that bring us the most meaning are those we choose with our hearts.

Of course, choosing with your heart doesn't always work out and isn't always the way to live. Sometimes the guy you traveled across the country to marry turns out to be a jerk. Sometimes your dream job that paid less money but you felt would be more rewarding turns out to be a nightmare. Sometimes when you gamble, you lose. When my wife and I were considering buying a house we loved but couldn't afford, I called my dad for advice. I told him that the house was perfect, would be a great investment over time, and although we really couldn't afford it everyone was telling me we should choke a little on our first house—really stretch our budget to the limit. To which my dad replied, "Steve, there's a difference between choking and lung cancer. Use your head. Don't buy the house."

He was right. Leading with our hearts won't always work out, at least not the way we'd hoped. For some of us, even if it would work out, it's hard to let go of the many ways in which we are raised and taught by society to be conventional and make the safe bet. The good news is that it is never too late to listen to your heart. Even once can change your life in a beautiful way. And, as someone who did follow her boyfriend across the country wisely noted, you needn't be afraid of the potential downside "as long as you understand the risks and are nimble enough to reorient yourself if need be." If you have already been fulfilled by a heartfelt choice, tell your loved ones about it so they too might be inspired to do the same.

Tell them not to worry about the cat either. At least not all the time.

What Makes You Happy?

Happiness is not a goal; it is a by-product.

—Eleanor Roosevelt

I once saw a grown man jump for joy. It happened during a small holiday party at his son's home. I was there under the guise of being a guest, but the truth was otherwise. Once all the invitees arrived, the man's son addressed the gathering. "I know you all think we invited you today because we were going to announce our engagement," he said, looking at the woman he had been dating for two years, "but you're wrong. We aren't getting engaged today." He paused to make sure all the air was out of everyone's emotional balloons and then, with impeccable timing, shouted, "We're getting married and here's the rabbi!" pointing at me. That was when I saw his father jump up and down, again and again, clapping his hands and shouting red-faced with joy, "Hooray!" The next thing you know, the groom flung open the hallway closet and pulled out a marriage canopy and six tuxedos for his father and friends. All the pants were too long, so I grabbed a stapler from the home office desk, stapled each pant leg to the right length, and we had ourselves a wedding. It was, in a word, perfect.

I will never forget witnessing the pure exuberance and transcendence of that sublime moment in that man's life. But was it really just a moment or was it something else?

We tend to think about happiness as a singular event or a spontaneous moment in time caused by external factors we do not control—a sort of lucky surprise, like winning the lottery without buying a ticket. But in most cases real happiness requires a process and is the distillate of mindful living day after week after month, and even after decades of intention. In other words, as opposed to pleasure, sudden and fleeting, happiness is the fruit of a slow-growing tree. That man was jumping for joy because that moment was not a moment, but instead, the result of decades' worth of the commitment, anxiety, frustration, laughter, and love that are parenting, the special bond of father and son forged over decades and the shared thrill of your child's happiness.

Even joyful moments that seem spontaneous are the result of careful planning and thoughtful living. That first kiss as spouses at a wedding, the tears and the joyful dancing throughout the night—these are most often the result of months of effort and agonizing with a wedding planner, caterer, florist, band leader, and others, and months or years of loving and caring for each other before that; moments grown, tended, and nurtured over time. It is a thoughtful, fully conscious life that results in joy, not the other way around. Or as one person so perfectly put it, "I do not sing because I am joyful. I am joyful because I sing."

But there is so much more to happiness than sustained effort over time. Happiness also depends upon others helping to create and share in our joy as we help create and share in theirs. The ancients realized they could be content alone, but not joyful. Yes, their peak moments were the result of hard work and careful planning, but also the result of communal pilgrimages, and the sacrifice of abundant produce and valuable animals at set times throughout the year. Not only was there nothing spontaneous about them, but there was also nothing ascetic or solitary about them either. Some of those sacrifices were given to the chief, shaman, priests, or prophets, others were offered up to deities on a fiery altar, but much was eaten in family groups. These were among the handful of times each year when ordinary people feasted on meat, clans and tribes gathering in massive, noisy, beautiful family reunions.

Most who answered this question about their own happiness proved not much has changed since antiquity. True happiness is communal. Life's most joyful songs cannot be sung solo. If it is not a shared experience, it is something other than happiness—contentment, momentary pleasure, hedonism perhaps, but not true happiness. Thanksgiving, Christmas, the Sabbath, birthdays, anniversaries, christenings, graduations, a great vacation—there is nothing solitary or spontaneous about them. We all crave solitude sometimes and the inner peace it can bring, but happiness is a heart-filled thrill we feel when we gather with others to celebrate an arrival after a long journey made with deeds of love and faith in the meaning of life.

There is a famous story about the violinist Isaac Stern, who was approached one evening after a concert by a fan. "Oh, Mr. Stern," the woman gushed, "I would give anything to be able to play the violin as beautifully as you do."

To which Stern replied, "Would you give ten hours a day?"

For those of us who seek joy, the sages and the answers to this question of happiness that you are about to read speak to the wisdom of investing time and love in the people closest to us. For only time and love shared in the company of others can imbue a moment with the singular, powerful, transcendent, and transformative jumping for joy that comes from knowing we have earned that moment the hard way.

❧

I love traveling up to Santa Barbara to have the dogs run free on Arroyo Burro Beach for miles on the white sands. Just to see them running with abandon in the surf with smiles on their faces and their joyful spirits on full display brings me a joy within I can't find anywhere else. My daughter also brings her pet rabbit, and she has him on a leash traipsing through the sands with us, and while it brings odd glances and expressions of surprise, for us it's pure heaven to have our animal family adventure with us in the wild.

Most of the things that have made me happy are not things at all, but experiences. Even when I've thought it was a "thing," when I actually unpack the joy, it's almost always in the use of the item, the sharing of it with someone else, and the feelings that are triggered in me.

Time with family and my small circle of friends makes me the happiest. And the small daily habits—meditation in my favorite chair, afternoon tea, a neighborhood walk with my husband.

I feel happiest when I am loving and serving others. The older I get, the more I realize that what comes from the heart, reaches the heart.

I have been raised to believe that real joy, true happiness, comes from bringing comfort or protection or sustenance or love to others.

The greatest unblemished happiness that I have ever experienced in my life was when my wife and I embraced each other after each of us had spent three weeks in the hospital with Covid. No satisfaction. No pride. No awe. Pure, unexpected happiness. When we embraced, no one, nothing else existed in the universe. Love? Of course. But an unexpected gift of life and sharing with the one person, the only person, around whom my life circles.

The lessons? Work hard for the things that truly matter. Don't sweat the rest. And choose the one you love as carefully as you can.

My happiest moments and my fondest memories are all about times with family and friends. I love thinking about the amazing family trips we took as children with my parents and the fun we had on them. I loved my wedding because I was with the man I loved most in the world, surrounded by so many people that loved me so much. Then there were the trips with my husband and then with our children that I recall so fondly. My fiftieth birthday away with my closest fifteen friends was a highlight. These are the memories that stand out to me as I age.

Have friends. Make new friends. Call and stay in touch with your friends.

The most important things are the most traditional things: building a home, having children, sharing afternoons with one another and with friends and family; the day-to-day activities that define relationships.

Almost all of the things that make me happy are things that money can't buy.

As an oncologist, when I have made a difference in someone's life (saved them, cured them, eased their suffering), I sometimes share this with my wife because I feel happy about it.

suffering), I sometimes share this with my wife because I feel happy about it.

Humor is humanity. Learn to love everyone, learn to laugh at everything (and everyone, especially yourself).

What makes me happy is working with partners I care for and respect. What makes me happy is going to sporting events, having meals, and going on walks with my closest friends. What makes me happy is having Passover, Thanksgiving, Break Fast, special events like bar and bat mitzvahs with my family and friends. What makes me happy is sharing the Super Bowl with people I enjoy sharing time with. What makes me happy is making a difference with people who have similar goals and beliefs.

It's so often the simplest things. A kind word at the right time, a walk in the woods, working hard on something and having it bear fruit. Basically, the lesson is to show up, be present, and keep it simple. The world is beautiful—let it show off for you.

Being with and sharing with family and good friends always makes me happy and reminds me that as you go through life, you really need to embrace relationships and treasure them.

Identifying the things that make you happy is the hard part. Once you know, you can make sure to carve out time for that in your life. It sounds clichéd to say life is short. But it is! I'm fifty-eight and my burger has flipped to the second side. Everyone knows how much faster a burger cooks once you flip it. Don't put off happiness.

Think about what you do every day and how you can tweak those things to make them more meaningful and yourself happier. Don't rely on a big vacation or a watershed event. Your life is made up of small moments. The small moments will add up to something much bigger than any one thing.

❧

I'm happiest when I'm less aware of myself. Happiest when I'm connecting with another person, heart to heart, soul to soul, guided by no motive other than joy.

❧

What makes you happy, and what lesson is there in the things that make you happy that you can share with your loved ones?

There is an old Chinese proverb about happiness that I try to remember each day. "If you want to be happy for an hour, take a nap. If you want to be happy for a day, go fishing. If you want to be happy for a month, get married. If you want to be happy for a year, inherit a fortune. If you want to be happy for a lifetime, help another person."

In order to find happiness, we have to find others for whom we make sacrifices born of love and with whom we share our lives. Happiness really is togetherness. It is who, not what, we have that makes us happy, and so often happiness is in the most ordinary moments with the ones we love. Tell the people you love about those moments great and small when happiness filled your heart because of them. Show them the way so that they too can find happiness now and when you are gone.

CHAPTER 4

What Was Your Biggest Failure?

I fell off my pink cloud with a thud.

—Elizabeth Taylor

It might have seemed like an insignificant moment, meaningless even, when I asked the famous Napa Valley chef Michael Chiarello about a problem I was having replicating my mother's chopped eggplant. I loved this Romanian dish from my childhood, especially spread thick on a piece of rye bread with a little salt on top. Years before, my mother had given me the old wooden bowl and chopper she used, along with her simple recipe and instructions. "Pierce a couple of large eggplants with a fork, place in the microwave until soft, scoop into a wooden bowl, and hand-chop until smooth. Add finely chopped onion, garlic powder, corn oil, and salt to taste."

As a boy, I loved the staccato *chop, chop . . . chop, chop, chop* that pulsed through the house and meant Mom's eggplant for lunch. I watched her make this dish for years as a kid and as an adult who wanted to learn when I knew that as she aged, her cooking days were coming to an end. But even after watching her for all those years, with her tools and recipe, when I tried to do the same thing, it never tasted exactly right. When I explained this to Chef Chiarello, he said, "Your mistake is watching your mother make it. She needs to watch you make it. You can't learn from watching someone else's success, only from a good teacher watching you fail."

There are a lot of stories about famous people who failed in order to succeed. After Fred Astaire's first screen test, the memo from the casting department at MGM said: "Can't act. Slightly bald. Can dance a little." Astaire framed the memo and kept it above his fireplace. Winston Churchill failed sixth grade. He didn't become prime minister of England until he was sixty-two, after a lifetime of political defeats. At an early job as a co-anchor at a local TV station in Baltimore, Oprah Winfrey was demoted. She found her passion for human-interest stories in the job she was demoted to, as a writer and reporter. Thomas Edison was called "too slow" by his elementary school teachers but went on, after two thousand attempts, to invent the light bulb. Lucille Ball was widely considered a failed movie actress before she made *I Love Lucy*. Babe Ruth held the record for the most strikeouts, in addition to being the home run king. And Michael Jordan didn't make his high school's varsity basketball team. As these legends would probably all agree, we cannot really succeed unless we learn first from failure.

I am not one to glorify failure and neither are the respondents to this question. I have regretted for years not seeking psychological help sooner to understand and undo the hurtful ways I often treated myself and others as a result of the harshness of my childhood. I am sorry I did not learn earlier that my success at work was often due to my own insecurities and the need to subordinate my anxiety rather than face it. It took too long for me to realize how, using workaholism to contain my anxiety, I was failing my wife and children. Sitting at the dinner table not long ago talking about a friend who was raising her children as a single parent, Betsy said matter-of-factly, "I was a single parent." How painful that was for me, and no doubt for her too. Failure hurts. It stings us and often those we care about. Failure is embarrassing and even shameful sometimes. It can take years to recover from and it is impossible to forget. But failure is a great teacher, attacking arrogance while inviting humility, painfully yet fortunately forcing us to take a cold, hard look at our own dysfunction, its roots and its thorns.

Whenever someone comes to see me to seek guidance after a moral failure, before I say a word I ask myself, where is this same core failure in my life? Had I never failed similarly I am not sure I would have any real ability to ease the suffering of the person in front of me or to guide them toward a better path. I am sure that being honest with myself about my own failures has made me a better, more humble, more empathetic, and less judgmental person. Nothing about recognizing and being honest about my failings has been easy, but failing does make it easier to forgive the failings of others. I have been harshly criticized for being as forgiving as I have been with people who have sinned and used that pain to change their lives. I am willing to accept that harsh critique because for me, given my own failures, my faith, and my role, there is no other way.

One of the best effects of being honest about our failures with the people we love is that it can prevent them from making the same mistakes, or at least encourage them not to wait to face a mistake and learn its lesson. Our truth can reduce the pain they would otherwise endure and inflict on others in ways we all too regrettably know we have done. I think Chef Chiarello was right. We don't learn nearly as much from trying to imitate another's success as we do from understanding our own failures.

Responding to this question, people were bravely and generously honest with me. I'm honored to pass on what they had to say about their failures. They have, with the benefit of hindsight, become their own teachers, watching their own past mistakes and learning some of life's most important truths. I hope their self-taught lessons acquired the hard way will inspire you to tell your own loved ones about yours.

~

Through much of my teens and (well) into my twenties, alcohol and drugs were at the center of my life. I lied, I broke promises, I drank myself sick more times than anyone could count, I was indiscriminate about who I was close to and how I was close to them. Most people who know me today know that I'm sober, but most of the people closest to me now didn't know me back then and would find it hard to believe just how often and how spectacularly I let everyone down, myself included. But it is undeniable that I wouldn't be the person I am today without every mistake, every humiliation, everything that I did and was done to me. I am genuinely grateful to have seen utter despair and to know what it is to be ashamed at my very core. Because knowing that gives me a depth of understanding and compassion that stands as a bulwark against my worst inclinations to judge or to look away from suffering when it makes me uncomfortable. I really know what it means to screw up, and have been given the grace to make amends and find a path out of self-hatred. So my greatest failings provide the building blocks for the best of who I am today.

I've lost my job twice. Even when the reason can be pinned to a recession, losing a job means losing your livelihood and your identity. It's also publicly humiliating. The first time I thought it was the end of my career. The second time I thought—wait a sec; I've been here before. So rather than have a gigantic freak-out, I kept my head down and took one step at a time. In fact, I had some interesting adventures along the way and wish now that I had paid more attention to them.

I was the younger of two children. I was the favored one. My sister was a lovely person, but she was not seriously interested in formal study. My parents celebrated my achievements and—though they loved her without any question—relegated my sister to every back seat accessible. And I happily, with full awareness, went along with the situation. My sister and I never grew apart, but we just failed to grow together. She married a man of a distinctly different social milieu. He traveled the carnival circuit. He printed and sold T-shirts. Often they lived in an RV. He was great to my sister and respectful to my parents.

I never reached out to them. No casual calls or brief notes. I once drove from New York to Atlanta, passing within fifty miles of their home—and did not stop.

Then my sister was dying. Her husband was already gone. She had an incurable blood disease. I went to see her only when she was within five days of death.

I judged her when I should have loved her. I ignored her when she was in the greatest need. I had fallen into a pattern that just set her off to the side.

How could I ever have treated my own sister that way? My wife and I, conscious of the past, have made it a singular goal to create settings and opportunities for our children and grandchildren to interact with each other, enjoy each other's company, and feel the power of family ties. This project has been superbly successful. But nothing changes the past.

❧

I didn't talk with a good college friend for a few years because of a boyfriend situation, and that argument was really wasted time. After Yom Kippur one year I reached out to her and we remain friends today. There is not much that can't be solved with a humble discussion and three simple words: "I am sorry."

～

Many years ago, I wronged a person for pretty much egocentric reasons. Years later I made an attempt to apologize, but from what I could gather, the person had died. Should you conclude you have hurt someone (intentionally or not), at least attempt to make amends as soon as possible.

～

By the time we reach our sixties, it's abundantly clear that we cannot distinguish our failures from what in hindsight—with lots of years to peer in the rearview mirror—was our good luck. I left Chicago after being refused tenure at Northwestern University. I migrated to California to accept some temporary teaching positions on two University of California campuses, then got a mid-career fellowship at the distinguished RAND Corporation, accepted a tenure-track position at the Cal State LA campus, became a full professor, and retired with emerita status and a really great pension!

My beloved goddaughter would never have been born had I stayed in Chicago. I would not have the cherished friends I made in California. I would not have a home with a white-water ocean view. I would not belong to the historic, beautiful Wilshire Boulevard Temple had I stayed in Chicago. I would not likely have a certain rabbi in my life were it not for my time in Chicago when he was my student in that ill-fated appointment at Northwestern. Or was it ill fated? On warm sunny days when I see images of snowstorms in Chicago, I realize what without doubt seemed like my bad luck at the time turned out to be my good luck.

❧

I tried for years to deny my true self. I tried to suppress my sexuality and got married twice. I especially regret getting married the first time, as I knew I should not be getting married. I believe it hurt my first wife and she has struggled her entire life to try and get past what I did to her.

I hope my loved ones will always be true to themselves and not try to be someone they are not, especially in relationships. It ends up hurting the other person and that is never a good thing.

❧

I think my biggest failure is that I was too busy at times to show my wife how much I love her.

~

I've been fired from jobs. I've had financial crises
and had to borrow money from friends. I work in
a field and in a profession where I encounter more
rejection in a year than most people face in a lifetime.
I suppose the lesson I've learned is not to take it
personally—most people's careers and lives are more
failure than success. And most people give up or change
directions, so stay the course and adapt to the
opportunities before you. You may just find yourself the
last person standing.

~

I literally left my dream job for a lesser, lighter position
because I felt I was going to be exposed as a fraud
unable to do the job. It was a seismic failure. This one
decision would derail my career for many years and
challenge my sense of self. I knew I had made a decision
based on a lie. For a brief moment I felt relieved the
pressure was off, but then deeply felt I had betrayed my
best self in taking the route of least resistance out of fear.
The lesson: Do it anyway. Be willing to fail to find out
who you are.

My biggest failure was not realizing early enough that in order to have a career you're passionate about, you have to get good at it. It doesn't happen magically. It takes practice and discipline. I only became good at my career in my late fifties.

I fail every day—often publicly and in big ways. But I have learned there really is no such thing as failure. No matter what you do, someone will say you failed. Don't amplify those voices or distill the positive reviews away. Don't let one person in a room prevent you from hearing the other nine who aren't loud critics. But stay humble and listen to the criticism and try to learn from it. Stick to your guns as long as you've consulted a lot of people first.

The things that make you most unpopular—as a parent, as a leader, as a friend—are sometimes the things that people remember you best for having done.

Finally, I would say this very simply: take the work seriously, but don't take yourself too seriously.

I've had so many failures, it's hard to just land on one. There is a teaching moment in all of them. Some took decades for me to understand. For instance, I didn't get into law school after college. This broke me. But what I didn't realize until years later was that I would have been a miserable lawyer. It simply wasn't the right career path for me.

A more recent failure that took place a few months ago taught me a great deal. I was slated to speak as a favor for a friend who had some major setbacks with Covid and business. I wanted to be there for him. But I somehow messed up the time in my calendar with Pacific Time instead of Central Time, and as I was prepping for the Zoom event I got a text that they were waiting for me. A flush of anxiety took me over. I got on the call quickly and was nowhere near as prepared as I wanted to be. I pulled through and yet I second-guessed everything I said inside my head as I spoke out loud. I felt like an awful failure and an embarrassment to my struggling friend. After the call, I wept for a long time. I hit the floor hard. For the next week, I was in tears and deeply disappointed. I apologized to my friend. He was gracious and understanding.

I eventually found the strength to watch the session I had led. I was shocked to see that it was not as bad as I had thought. Finally, I understood why my friend was still grateful for my efforts. I still scratch my head when I think of this moment. How could my read of my contribution have been so off? Sometimes we let our judgments run amok inside our heads. Sometimes our own desire to succeed undermines our very confidence. The lesson for me in this experience is to just keep showing up and investing in people you love. Keep trying. When you mess up, don't beat yourself up. Find a way to make it right and move forward.

As crazy as this sounds to say, I don't actually look back on any particular "great failures," at least not at this point in my life. I have always generally felt that failures are important opportunities to learn and grow. And I think that's what I would share with my loved ones. Failure can bring disappointment and embarrassment, and sometimes consequences that have to be addressed. But if you can get past those, you can walk away changed, grown, and improved by the experience.

My biggest failure is not always hearing other people when I am sure that I am right. I have engaged in loud, passionate (some say angry) diatribes rather than reasoned dialogue. I think that I can see into the future and how things will or will not work out and I give in to my ego and my hurts.

Simply put, my relationship with my father.

He was uneducated. Knew nothing about sports and had no real interest to learn. He never went to any of my games because he was too busy working for our family. He was not a good husband. But when I reflected about our relationship, right after his death, I realized my dad was the one person who gave my brother and me unconditional love.

That was just not enough. I wanted a dream dad. Sending me to the best schools, and always telling me how special I was, was not good enough for me. He was an older dad (ironically, just like I turned out to be), but virtually all my friends had younger dads. Another reason to be embarrassed about my dad.

My greatest flaw, in my view, is I could not accept my

dad, who was an uneducated man damaged by his poverty-stricken upbringing, a survivor of the Holocaust who lost his first family. He was not the flawed one, I was.

My deepest failure: not realizing this when my dad was alive. Not realizing sooner that I am a much better, more confident person as the man he helped raise. He always made it clear I could do anything I set my sights on, even in my most insecure times. I just wish when my dad had dementia and said at the age of ninety-three that he didn't think I loved him, and I said I did, that I meant it at that time. I do now! I could keep writing about my relationship with my dad, and how I let it go so off the rails, but I want to stop crying because it is something I cannot fix.

❧

What was your biggest failure and what lesson did you learn that is worth sharing with your loved ones?

A lot of people think the hardest thing to say is "I'm sorry," but I think it is even harder to say, "I was wrong." It's hard to say those words to others and often even harder to ourselves. At some point every one of us has been punished for being wrong rather than encouraged for trying. We all spend a lot of time in our lives pretending we have not erred in ways immoral, foolish, unkind, or simply human. That denial and withholding of the truth about our lives keeps terrible feelings bottled up within us and robs others of the opportunity to learn from our mistakes as we hopefully have. In nearly every example, reckoning came far later than people wished. Here again, the simple message seems to be "Don't wait."

Not long ago I was interviewed on a podcast about my last book, about how failing to overcome our fear of death prevents us from fully living. The podcast focused on various taboos in Western culture, and during the conversation the host said something simple and profound: "If we can talk about it, we can manage it." That has been so true in my life. It is the things I do not talk about with the people I love and trust that cause me the most pain and regret. Talking about our failures is good for us. It relieves the pressure of keeping a secret or denying our foolish, even bad behavior. It is also good for the people we care about. It humanizes us and sets an important example of self-scrutiny, honesty, and vulnerability.

The columnist David Brooks points out that the people he admires most have reckoned with their "core sin" by identifying it and then humbly trying to correct the bad behavior that resulted from it. Take some time to consider your greatest failure and what lesson lives within it. This may well be the most important truth and invaluable gift you can bequeath to the ones you love.

CHAPTER 5

What Got You Through Your Greatest Challenge?

You should never view your challenges as a disadvantage. Instead, it's important for you to understand that your experience facing and overcoming adversity is actually one of your biggest advantages.

—**Michelle Obama**

One of my favorite jokes involves a fire in a small town. Everything in the center of the town is in flames and the heat is so intense that none of the fire engine companies can get close enough to fight the fire. The only thing they can do is encircle the town and watch it burn. Suddenly, from a distance through the thick smoke, comes one lone fire truck at high speed, continuing past all the other fire trucks. Amazingly, the truck rolls to a stop right in the heart of the fire. It turns out it's the fire truck from the local convent. Everyone watching is shocked as nuns start jumping out of the truck in a frenzy, hopping around like frenetic fleas with axes, hoses, and ladders. To everyone's surprise and delight, the fire is out in ten minutes and the town is saved.

The next week the town organizes a parade to thank the nuns. At the end of the festivities the mayor invites the Mother Superior onto the stage and hands her a check for ten thousand dollars as a thank-you from the town's citizens. A news reporter is there who shouts, "Mother Superior, what are you going to do with the money?"

To which she replies, "The first thing I am going to do is fix the brakes on that fucking truck!"

It's a great joke, but it also reveals a difficult truth. Sometimes we are the cause of our own misfortune, but other times, we are in a fight we never asked for and do not deserve. At some point we all face terribly sad and difficult challenges through no fault of our own. There is much to learn about courage and humility from those who have fought the deserved and undeserved fires of searing adversity.

When someone's life falls apart, I am often their first call. "Steve, the story just broke and there are pictures too. I am so ashamed. I don't know what to do." "Steve, Ron just shot himself in the basement. Can you meet us at the hospital right away?

Please?" "Steve, I just found out Ella is cheating on me with another dad at school. I'm devastated." "Steve, Carrie died in her sleep last night and I don't know how to tell the girls. My God, they're so young . . . Please come." "Steve, I need you to testify for me as a character witness. I am so afraid. I wish I was dead." "Steve, the coroner is finished and the funeral is Friday. We just can't carry that tiny casket with our beautiful baby girl inside. Will you?" (The names are changed but these are all real examples.)

Of course, none of this is easy for me. But before heading out the door I always try to remind myself how much more difficult it is to be the person suffering than the one on his way to help. And when I arrive, my counsel is based on lessons I have learned from watching so many others walk through hellish fires and from my own battles with suffering. That counsel is based on three basic realizations confirmed by my own experience and by everyone who has answered this question. The first is illustrated well in the following true story that I read on a website devoted to medical matters. This one is no joke:

I cannot tell you my name, or where I live, or even the specialty within which I practice medicine. I cannot do so for I have been shamed, embarrassed, and at times stigmatized. Even today, years later, I fear retribution, liability, and even prosecution. Some of this may have been deserved at one time, but today my story is one of success. It is a story of hope, of support and of recovery. I share this intimate tale so that you, my colleagues and friends in the medical field, can hear the human side of addictive disease, of its treacherous grip, and of the freedom and confidence from which I have emerged from this terrifying illness.

My drug use did not begin until medical school. I was never a drinker in high school or even in college, nor did I use drugs socially. Then, one evening when I was finding it hard to stay awake to study for an organic chemistry exam, a friend directed me to some stimulants that were available in sample form. The result was perfect. I began using the pills, rather innocently, whenever I needed a boost. To me, it was like a cup of coffee, only better. I soon learned that I could order the pills on the Internet and have a supply whenever it was needed.

Upon graduation, I entered practice determined to be the best doctor possible. I spent a great deal of time with my patients, who kept coming back. My patient load grew exponentially, and I had trouble keeping pace. I had no experience running a business, was working long hours, and was unable to juggle the growing load. I found myself taking more and more pills just to keep up, and then even more pills to get me to sleep again. . . .

My drug use escalated. In addition to Internet orders I would write prescriptions in the names of my family members. Suddenly, my uncle had knee pain, my father-in-law back problems, my aunt arthritis. I did not think about the record I was establishing of their purported use, nor did I think about the records of my own prescribing practices. I was out of control, but getting by, taking many pills to get through each day.

Throughout this time I still felt on top. Despite my drug use, I was a physician with a thriving practice. I provided quality care and had no patient complaints. I had a wife and children that relied upon me and saw me as a great provider. My friends and family admired me. I was respected in the community. I enjoyed my status and felt it was deserved, having achieved academically as well as socially since childhood.

And then one day, the Drug Enforcement Agency came to the door inquiring about fraudulent prescriptions. The reality of the situation took months to sink in. My reaction was disbelief. I was no druggie engaged in covert activities, and I was certainly no criminal. I was an admired and respected physician. I was sure the entire misunderstanding would be cleared up with a smile and an apology. I could not have been more wrong.

The shame and magnitude of my tumble was immeasurable. Not only did I face the legal and professional ramifications of having written improper prescriptions, but I had to cope with the personal humiliation of a fall from grace. I was no longer the icon of success I had worked a lifetime to achieve. I was now tainted, not only in the eyes of my colleagues, but also, for the very first time, in my own.*

This is a cautionary tale for all of us, not only about the insidious power of addiction, but also the dangers of denial. This physician had to know on some level that his drug use and writing of bogus prescriptions were problematic. He seems to have shut out that awareness in order to keep rationalizing the stupendous risks he was taking with his health, his career, his patients, and his family. Imagine how his story could have turned out if, say, at the moment before filling the first illegal script, he had instead sought help for his addiction. Being on the inside of so many people's lives, and of course my own, has shown me again and again that we all have these missed opportunities when denial, ego, fear, or shame prevent us from facing our

---

* https://www.massmed.org/Physician_Health_Services/Helping_Yourself_and
_Others/A_Personal_Story_of_Addiction/.

moral failures and cause the resulting consequences to be so much worse later on.

One of the things people often say to me about my writing is that I allow myself to be vulnerable in a way that is generally unexpected from clergy. Why am I willing to share my faults and failures despite being thought of as a moral exemplar? For the same reason that I hope that you will share yours with your loved ones. Your experience can pierce the denial and encourage the people you care about to face their problem the first time they cheat, the first time they feel a lump, or dark depression, or lie about some compulsion getting the better of them. At the very least your vulnerability can lessen their loneliness, shame, and fear because someone they love and admire has also made mistakes. Telling the truth about our painful lapses in judgment bestows a healing legacy upon the people we love most. Other than wine and teenagers, who eventually grow up, very few things get better with time. The sooner we confront our problems the better. What a gift if our truth-telling leads our loved ones to the relief we felt when we finally faced our demons, but sooner and with less pain.

The second realization many of us have had from adversity is the importance of reaching out. It takes a lot of maturity to let others know we are suffering. So many of us are taught from a young age that real courage comes from going it alone, that needing help is cowardly and weak. And yet, we know that no one suffers pain better alone, no one! From all of the pain I have witnessed others endure and from my own, I think the worst part of it is the feeling of isolation and abandonment, that sense that no one can or should help us and that no one else really cares or understands. It took me many years to learn my pain is halved when I share it with someone I trust. Going it alone is a long, unnecessarily difficult journey. As I have quoted many times before, the sages of the Talmud said, "The prisoner cannot free himself." That is such a wise reminder that when we are suffering, reaching out to others will liberate us from our isolation and diminish our pain.

Finally, the most important thing to know about life's greatest and most painful challenges is that we do somehow endure them and learn to live and love more fully because of them. This is not to say that these challenges are worth the pain, merely that they are ultimately not worthless if they ennoble us with a greater sense of gratitude for all that we still have and for what we have learned. I have seen the parents of a dead child eventually living, laughing, and loving again despite the sorrow that will always be there. I have heard a judge in federal court assure a man that he would be able to endure prison and still have a meaningful and wonderful life afterward. I recently saw the man in question and the judge was right. I have seen a woman who lost both of her breasts to cancer and then had to correct botched reconstruction surgery laughing, swimming, and loving again. I have stood beneath the wedding canopy with widows who have fallen in love again. A man who suffered a terrible business failure and was unable to fulfill a million-dollar pledge he had made to our congregation called me several years later to say, "I am back on my feet and want to make good on that pledge."

Sooner or later we are all wounded and scarred, often badly, in ways ugly and frightening. Yet we have a remarkable ability to survive, heal, and grow in the aftermath of life's most terrible blows. Join my friends here in sharing your most difficult challenges and how you have overcome them, learned from them, and made peace with them. Your faith, your truth, your courage, and your self-compassion are powerful lessons for your loved ones who need you now by their side when they are in pain and by their side too even when, especially when, you are gone.

❧

I have always had a strong personality. I can be confrontational, which can sometimes rub people the wrong way. But in the case of the defining moment of my life, a car accident where I caused someone's death, I couldn't have predicted how my personality would help me. But it did. I don't know how I got through that challenging time. There was no prescription. No steps written down to tell me what to do. I just tried to face the truth. I accepted that I couldn't control the event, but I could control how I behaved afterward. If you spend time brooding over why me, why did this happen, you stay a victim. I think facing the facts, looking into the fire, so to speak, is the only way to get through to the other side. Today's me, ten years out from that tragedy, would like to tell my loved ones that no matter how bad it gets, the pain won't last forever.

My greatest challenge has been not having my mom and dad there in certain moments in my life. This is why I am trying my best to be a great mother.

A busy schedule is what gets me through. I mean it. Having to show up and go to work the next hour, minute, or day. Force yourself to keep going and before you know it, that terrible thing has receded or something new has come about and things you felt would never go away, or were impassable, suddenly have passed.

My greatest challenge in life has been my battle with alcoholism and addiction. Even though I was able to stop drinking and was relieved of the physical obsession to drink when I was twenty-six, the "ism" of alcoholism broke through from time to time causing great emotional pain, and during my relapse, horrible physical and spiritual pain.

I believe that "willingness" saved my life:

Willingness to be honest, even when I was sure that being honest would cause people to cast me aside.

Willingness to attempt to have a daily contact with God through prayer.

Willingness to attempt to see my part in any situation where resentment, hurt, and anger reside.

Willingness to tell my struggles to the people who care about me regardless of how I will look to them.

Willingness to "look weak" and ask people for help.

Willingness to dive back into Alcoholics Anonymous and try to do the program as best I can.

Adversity has made me stronger, and I welcome the opportunities that adversity gives me. I connect to God, my higher self, and my soul in order to push forward and break down doors, walls, and windows that stand in my way of serving God. I have broken down these same doors, windows, and walls for the sake of me at times and this has always brought pain, failure, and damage.

I would remember what my mother and my grandmother had been through—sometimes on my watch—and I'd think, "If she can get through that, I can get through this." I can't emphasize strongly enough that whatever is happening, you will come out the other side. You don't even have to make it happen. Time will pass without your pushing it.

My family. My love for the Jewish people. My total embrace of the imperative not only to heal our world but to help set the world in an increasingly positive direction. Of course I will fall short. But the effort, the need to try, is exhilarating. And somehow I keep on finding teachers, superb, brilliant people, who open additional gates of wisdom for me.

Something within that I cannot explain. I have always been internally guided to move forward, to deal with the challenge at hand, to figure out solutions and to move on. Not holding on to the bad things that happen in life is so important.

Don't be afraid to ask for help. There are plenty of people out there who want to help you and can help you. It makes them feel good to do so.

I had achieved lots of success in my career but had difficulty finding real love. I had had a difficult childhood and the models of relationships for me were not the healthiest. You attract the love you think you deserve, I'm told, or that which is most familiar. When I finally found love and got married late in life, it was devastating to realize it was not a marriage that would last. This was a time in my life where everything seemed to be falling apart despite my greatest hope and efforts. Not only was my relationship dying on the vine, but I had given up my career to build a family at last, and then my husband lost his job. I felt shame and embarrassment to be in such a difficult financial predicament, and was also deeply ashamed I could not fix it or make it better. I was battling severe depression and a sense of hopelessness and failure. I had no idea how to climb out of this hole, but I knew I had to. I had adopted a child with my husband and so wanted to make this family work and find the sanctuary I had always longed for; but when it became clear things would not change, I knew what I needed to do. It was the love and hope for my daughter and a deep commitment not to repeat the challenges of my own childhood that forced me to find the strength and courage to break free and rebuild my life. It was the hardest thing I'd ever done. What literally propelled me through was my love and dreams for my little girl. It was not about me or my wants. It was about the life I wanted to model and build for my child.

I first made a plan, made clear I needed to break free from a spiraling relationship that could not be fixed by me. I then strategized a way back into the workforce and, by the grace of God, found my way home. What I would advise my daughter in times that challenge every atom of your being is to first identify the values you most hold dear and ask yourself if you are living in alignment with those values. If you come to the conclusion your life is out of alignment, make a plan to realign your life so you are congruent in every way.

∼

Faith. Family. Friends. Having something to believe in that is greater than I am always gave me the confidence to keep on walking. When we are completely overwhelmed, it is good to know that God sees your situation; he knows and he cares. Ours is in the trying, the rest is not our business. While it is true that we can choose our friends but not our family, I am eternally grateful for both. Over time, you realize that they are what matter most.

~

Know the difference between adversity and disappointment, a heartbreak and a bummer. Keeping a sense of perspective has always been what has gotten me through life's challenges. It is difficult to count our blessings when we're in the midst of trauma, but there are always blessings. Give yourself time to grieve, to lick your wounds. Never discount your real feelings of pain and loss, but also don't lose yourself in them.

~

The intense bond I had with my dad for the fifteen years we were together enabled me to withstand his death and move on in my life. Losing my dad in a plane crash when I was a teenager so far has been my greatest challenge. However, having to face such a tragedy at such a young age made me grow up very quickly. I felt very much alone. My dad was my everything, but I learned that, as humans, we're very strong and can handle a lot. Even though he was gone physically, I've felt spiritually—and still do forty-two years later—that my dad is a part of my heart and mind always.

Advice: Keep the values of the loved ones you've lost as your guiding light. Be grateful for what you have and had. Surround yourself with people who have your back and truly love you. Try to be the person that the people who truly love you think you can be. Lastly, don't rush yourself. Faced with adversity, take your time and take care of yourself.

❧

I dug deep, leaned on family and friends and faith, read inspirational books, sought advice of clergy, and accepted help.

❧

Keeping a connection with God has helped me through so many challenges. I have spent many hours with my head to the ground on my prayer rug praying for guidance. All while specifically thinking of this verse from the Quran: "Celebrate the glory of your Lord and be among those who bow down to God: worship your Lord until what is certain comes to you." (15:98–99)

Prayer has been my saving grace while feeling overwhelmed by grief, when I moved to new places and felt alone, and more recently with so much fear and uncertainty regarding Covid-19. God's mercy and love are infinite. When I put my trust in the Almighty, eventually my path ahead becomes clear.

～

My father used to say that religion was only for people who needed support to make it through tough times, implying that, if you had been forged in the crucible of suffering, there would be no need for religion. But for me, organized prayer in a worship service gave me an insight into what the therapists refer to as mindfulness. There is nothing that requires more attention, for a Reform Jew, than learning the daily prayers in Hebrew, in a live (not Zoom) minyan, and then being asked to lead those prayers. It requires attention to minute detail, it requires acceptance of daily mistakes, it requires sufficient humility to ask questions, and all that takes you away from your obsessive self. Prayer is focused, it is directed, and it is detailed, and I suspect it changes, however briefly, the chemistry of the mind.

Growing up, my greatest challenge and the major cause of my insecurity was my eyesight. When I was a young boy, my glasses were thick. I was terrified that I would be asked in school to read from the blackboard or something projected on the screen, and when I could not do that I would be embarrassed in front of my classmates. I was fiercely competitive, but my hand-eye coordination sucked.

I dreaded going through life handicapped by my lousy eyesight. I decided to make my greatest fear and challenge a positive instead of a negative. I worked as hard as I could to train my brain to let me present with no more than notes, if even that. While I didn't have a great basketball shot, I compensated for that limitation by focusing on defense. I knew I had a challenge, but I was not going to let my disability destroy me. Today I still do not have perfect eyesight, but because of the wonders of medicine and cataract surgery I can see so much better.

I have worked hard to teach my loved ones to see problems as opportunities. Rather than let adversity destroy you, if at all possible, you need to allow it to make you stronger.

Straight on. Just face it!

Make a plan. Do not ignore, deny, or delay. It's not going to go away. I try to only keep counsel with those whom I know to have experience, good guidance, and to not judge.

Truly in any time in my life that seems impossible I lean into my faith. God is good and He will take all of your burdens on His shoulders. Give your worries and troubles to Him so that you walk a lighter road.

It's always been the kindness and insight I've gained from other people that have gotten me through—sometimes family or friends, but often people I've barely known, i.e., the kindness of strangers. On my own, I face adversity with sheer force of will and determination, but that only allows me to tread water, not to get anywhere in the open ocean. It is only when I open myself up to another human being, and risk that they might find out that I'm not perfect (which was an open secret), that I have made the shifts and transformation necessary to move through the most difficult passages in my life. A little light, a little humor, some empathy, some wisdom—they all have allowed me to find a way through the worst of times.

~

What enabled you to withstand and move on in the face of your greatest challenge? What advice can you offer your loved ones to guide them when they encounter real adversity?

In my thirties I participated in an age circle with one hundred men, ages twenty-five to eighty-five. We created the circle standing shoulder to shoulder, beginning with the youngest man in the group, then the next oldest, and the next and the next until all one hundred of us were in order. Once the circle was complete, each man got to ask the men across from him a question. Those men on the opposite side of the circle were roughly thirty years older or younger than the person asking the question. This meant I was able to seek the advice of men twice my age. I decided to ask them about what they knew in their sixties that they wish someone had told them in their thirties. One man, whose son was killed in a car crash while his daughter was driving, despite him having told their mother not to allow the daughter to drive because conditions were too dangerous, said,

"You can survive almost anything." The room was silent. What he didn't say was how. Hopefully the answers of others have helped you consider your own inner strength, your own "how" when you have faced real and painful adversity. Speak about your how. It will bestow courage and strength across the circle of your life to those left behind with their own struggles when you are gone.

CHAPTER 6

What Is a Good Person?

There is zero chance of being a good person
without doing good for others!

—Mehmet Murat Ildan

My wife and I visited Paris in January. It was cold, windy, and wet, yet somehow still beautiful, as only Paris can be. Shivering and tired, we stepped into a fancy hotel to warm up and have a snack. Soft music wafted through the perfumed air in the polished, marble-clad lobby. Even in winter, there were flowers everywhere, handsome men and beautiful, seemingly carefree women with Hermès bags slung over their arms making their way toward the plush taupe chairs in the café off to the side.

After we ordered our coffee and croissants, I googled this magical place. The Hôtel Lutetia was built in 1910. Its famous guests over the years have included Pablo Picasso, Charles de

Gaulle, André Gide, Peggy Guggenheim, and Josephine Baker. James Joyce wrote part of *Ulysses* there.

Things changed when the Nazis occupied Paris in June of 1940 and requisitioned the hotel. They used it to house, feed, and "entertain" the officers in command of the occupation. Suspected collaborators were tortured in a prison across the street so the torturers could easily make it back to the hotel in time for tea. Survivors were housed there immediately after the war. When de Gaulle met the first of them and heard what they had endured, he wept.

I felt so strange nibbling on my perfect, flaky croissant and sipping a cappuccino in that terrible, beautiful place. So it is, I thought, with buildings, places, and people. We are all so many things . . .

The complicated truth is that the question of good and evil is not about our essence but about our essence at any given moment. Ask anyone fighting to stay sober one day, one hour, one minute at a time. Ask anyone in a committed relationship with a wandering eye deciding whether or not to remain his or her best and truest self. Ask anyone who has ever felt tempted by anything, eaten of the apple, and then felt shame. When it comes to good and evil, we are each at the center of a battle that sometimes rages and sometimes smolders within us until we die. In the words of Soviet-era dissident Aleksandr Solzhenitsyn (who survived the gulag by eating rats and knew a good deal more than most about evil), "If only there were evil people somewhere insidiously committing evil deeds, and it were necessary only to separate them from the rest of us and destroy them. But the line dividing good and evil cuts through the heart of every human being."

Religion tends to oversimplify good and evil in terms of heaven and hell. You end up in one or the other, never both. But when we really look inside ourselves, we see that heaven or hell is a far more complicated matter than us or them, and up or down. Consider this seemingly simple story that is anything but. With slight variations, it has become part of the folklore of several cultures, including Hindu, Buddhist, Muslim, Jewish, and Christian. This version of the story is attributed to Rabbi Haim of Romshishok.

A man wants to know the secrets of heaven and hell. God grants his wish and sends him a guide to escort him first to hell. They enter a large room in a beautiful palace. The residents of hell are seated around a banquet table. Golden platters are piled high with the most delicious food imaginable. But none of the food has been touched. The emaciated dinner guests moan from the constant ache of hunger. "If these people are so hungry why don't they eat?" the man asks his guide.

"Look closely," the guide replies. "They have no elbows. Their arms are locked straight in front of them.

They can't bend their arms to bring the food to their mouths."

Next, the guide takes the man up to heaven, where they enter a banquet room identical to the one they just visited in hell. And the diners had the same unbendable arms as those in hell, but everyone was fed and happy. "What gives?" the visitor asks his guide. "Why are these people so happy if they can't help themselves to the food?"

"Look more closely," the guide tells the man. He does and realizes that each person is lifting his or her stiff, unbending arms to feed the person across the table.

The story challenges us to ask why people in hell behave differently. Don't the people there want to be fed too? Of course they do. If everyone in heaven and everyone in hell wants to eat, that means hell lacks something heaven does not. That something is the ability to care about others who are starving too.

Hell is the place where people do not care about other people. And that hell sometimes exists inside each of us. Why do I sometimes give money to the homeless woman who offers to wash my windshield at the gas station but other times look away? Because like all of us for whom empathy comes and goes, I am sometimes in heaven and sometimes in hell. There are moments of light, many of them, when I can feel so keenly the suffering of others, and moments, many of them, when I am in a dark too dark to see and can think only of myself.

Schopenhauer asked this question. How is it that an individual can respond to the pain and suffering of another as though it were his own pain and suffering? How is it that an individual can forget her own safety and fly to the help of another at the risk of her own life? Schopenhauer's answer is that compassion is the experience of a truth that you and that other are one. That the experience of separateness is secondary. And deeper than that, all life is one life, all consciousness one consciousness, and when we help another human being, we affirm the oneness of us all.

We all know who reached out when we were suffering alone and afraid, who showed up with a meal, a note, a hug, a ride, a laugh. We all know compassion when we feel it. We all know goodness when we see it. And we all know it depends upon whether or not each of us wins the war within us again and again and again. The misery in the world and in our families, all of it stems from the simple but terrible temptation we have, often many times a day, to take and not to give, to shout rather than to listen, to believe the hearts and souls of others are different and less complicated, less human than our own, and that whether they are people who look very different from us and live far away or they are our own family, somehow if we prick them, they do not bleed—and if we do not acknowledge them , they do not matter. We live in a world where it is so easy to objectify the other and where the answer for each of us to the question "Do you care; do you really care about other people?" is neither yes nor no, but sometimes.

The first law of biology is self-protection. The first law of the spirit is compassion. Yes, these can come into conflict, but it is compassion that makes us more than animals. Compassion is what defines goodness. Compassion is heaven on earth. You can see the power and beauty of compassion running through the answers I gathered to this question, "What is a good person?"

Being a good person is to know that what you do has an impact on other people. It is not necessarily a matter of being totally selfless, but rather holding the simultaneous ideas that we are responsible for ourselves and our happiness, and that the happiness of others is equally important.

Being a good person is taking the next right action that serves God and others. Being a good person is being in action to "love your neighbor as yourself"; it is caring for the stranger, the poor, the needy, the powerless, and the voiceless in oneself and in another.

My grandfather used to always tell me that I did not necessarily have to be "good" to anyone, but that I had to be "fair" with everyone. That always stuck with me. We get to decide who we want to be especially good to, but we have to be fair with everyone. At a minimum, being fair with others is the standard for being a good person. The higher standard? Wanting (and working) for everybody else's child to have access to the very same things that you would want for your child.

It's hard to describe what a "good person" is, but you absolutely know it when you are with them! I know I live with one. He's stand-up, kind, strong, considerate, doesn't care about people's bank accounts or how "important they are," does the right thing, and wants no recognition for it.

A good person is one who is willing to pause when they are wronged. To listen more deeply and think about how or what others need to become their better selves. Sikh activist and author Valarie Kaur describes this as revolutionary love. I find that I am more aware of this when I fast during Ramadan. The lack of food and water during the day compounded by sleep deprivation from nightly and early morning prayers slows me down just enough that I pay more attention to the subtleties that allow me to see what others are communicating and needing. The thirty-day fast is hard and a tool to refine one's character. If only we would submit to it and get past our hangry moments that lead us into mistreating others. Our inner goodness comes through when the body is no longer in charge of our actions and our self-restraint allows us to imagine the good we can do around us. In chapter 5 on fasts in the Mishnah, the text reminds us to remember past events of hardship, reflect on them, and fast. When we do so, we "return to goodness." There are many paths in different traditions to goodness. Choose one. It is a hard journey that is worth every step. Being a good person is not a superficial state of being. It is an intense path toward your better self.

Consistently trying to do your best, whatever that is and at whatever level you are able. The key words are *consistently*, because you will not always do it, and *trying*, because you will not always hit the mark. It's not a perfection contest. But you have to set the bar high and keep at it.

~

I love the patterns and templates established by the movement of Jewish ethical behavior known as Mussar. Immediate pleasure, instant gratification, thoughtless decision-making cannot ever be constitutive elements of what a good person might be. Goodness requires practice and effort and focus.

A good person can never be a Dorian Gray person. What we do impacts us. We can scar and cripple our souls by the choices we make.

A good person will subsume some of their personal needs so that the greater community can receive a greater good. Goodness requires maturity. Goodness requires autonomy. Goodness requires a personal set of standards that are ever pasted onto the mirror of our lives. Goodness never requires perfection, but always requires a willingness to acknowledge where we have fallen short.

Goodness can be defined by what we hope to see in the behavior of our children and grandchildren.

Giving of oneself—volunteering, whether to friends or family in need, or a charity—giving time, money, self. Saying thank you to those that help you, whether it's the person at the checkout stand or someone who helps in a more significant way.

A good person shows up and is there for others. A good person stands up for themselves and for others.

Ethics are situational, morals are static. A good person can do bad things—but doing certain bad deeds means you are no longer a good person. A good person sets boundaries. A bad person crosses those boundaries one too many times. (*Kadosh, kosher,* all come from the word for "setting apart"—so setting boundaries can be holy.)

I think when you are a good person you are radiating love. Love is everything. Goodness is love.

To be loving, understanding, and to be there when you are needed.

The good person will sacrifice personal interest to the benefit of the greater community. This implies having a strong sense of empathy and concern for others, and a willingness to act when the situation warrants.

I never lie to my kids or cheat on my taxes. But if I needed to lie to protect my family, such as many Jews did during the Holocaust, then I would without question. And I'd still consider myself a good person.

A good person cares for others. A good person is sympathetic. A good person is generous. A good person can laugh at him- or herself. A good person enjoys helping others. And a good person doesn't need a reminder to do good things.

Active silence. By this I mean that, however much I would like to say something, there are moments when, out of compassion, it would be better to be silent. I guess that that means being merciful when someone vulnerable has hurt you. I am not always that good person; I am not so virtuous, but silence can be aspirational if you can avoid internalizing hurt. I guess that the general rule is the categorical imperative of not doing to someone what you would not wish to have done to you.

A good person: 1. Treats people at least as well as they expect to be treated. 2. Tries to be nice to everyone. Rich or poor, smart or of middling intelligence, we all put our pants on one leg at a time. 3. Gives back. Whatever your community or nonprofit passion, give back. 4. Helps people be better, rather than wishes them ill. 5. Is honest with people, except when you may hurt their feelings. White lies are okay. Other lies are not. 6. Does not gossip or bad-mouth anyone, particularly their friends. This may be the hardest quality to maintain in being a good person. 7. Makes people smile and be happy. How hard is it to say hello, thank you, you look great, can I help you with anything? 8. Is someone people usually want to be around.

For me, being a good person means asking how can I authentically serve. Service through kindness, compassion, support, companionship, empathy, and presence.

～

I think being a good person is living a conscious and conscientious life. For me, it means being able to sleep at night, knowing I've made the best decisions I could with the information I had available. It means being compassionate toward others and myself. And it means appreciating that we are all part of something much bigger than ourselves (likely more than one "something").

～

I think it's honesty, authenticity, generosity, mindfulness. Balancing taking care of yourself while also having the ability to put others first when it's appropriate and always showing up.

～

The Golden Rule: do unto others as you wish unto you. What is a good person? This is such a loaded question because it implies good and evil when the aspiration is much larger than that duality. Being good for me means showing up and trying my best even when I'm tired or my ego is bruised. It means getting up in the middle of the night when you have a big project due the next day, but your kid needs to talk to you. It means being kind when you are angry and generous when you feel slighted. Patience is a large part of goodness and so is a willingness to own up to failure and bad behavior, mistakes and missteps. Being good is being present to yourself and trying to walk your talk no matter what assails you on the path.

❧

A good person gives and forgives, has a moral compass that realizes we are all equal in not being perfect. Struggle is good; it makes us compassionate. It's like the ocean's calm or roar, being perpetually pulled by the earth's gravitation one way or the other to keep us balanced and not complacent.

❧

What does it mean to be a good person?

"At the moment of conception," says the Talmud, "an angel takes the drop of semen from which the child will be formed and brings it before God. 'Master of the Universe, what shall be the fate of this drop?' asks the angel. 'Will it develop into a strong person or a weak one? A wise person or a fool? A wealthy person or a poor one?' Whether the person will be wicked or righteous, this he does not ask."

Why not? Why doesn't the angel ask God if the soon-to-be-formed person will be wicked or righteous? Because the sages believed we—not our genetic makeup, not our environment, not even God—are responsible for our moral choices. The genetic fix might be in when it comes to how tall or how strong we will be, perhaps even how intelligent we might be, but not how decent we might be. Our decency is up to us.

Here's some good news. Behaving ethically and morally—being kind, truly kind—helps others around us be more kind. Consider the research project in which a person stood next to a car with a flat tire in a residential area of Los Angeles. Passing motorists who had seen someone helping another person change a tire a quarter of a mile back were almost twice as likely to stop and help than were those who had not driven by the previous helping scene.

Helpful, generous people inspire. They are reminders of the choices we have before us. They invite our compassion to emerge. Just imagine for a moment that you and the people you love most are standing behind a line drawn in the sand. Those who choose to cross the line to the other side commit themselves to fairness, kindness, sensitivity, and compassion. No one is moving. Everyone is held back by vulnerability, fear, self-interest, or indifference. If you step over the line, perhaps they will follow you. But they need your inspiration.

Once, while sitting in the dining room of my father's nursing home, I struck up a conversation with a volunteer. He was an important attorney who was retired. To fill his time, he volunteered a couple of days a week as an ombudsman at the home. It was his job to handle complaints and be an advocate for the residents and their families.

"When someone from the community sees me here I know what they are thinking," he told me. "'He used to be an important person at the highest levels in business and politics, a dealmaker, and now here he is volunteering at this nursing home.'

"But do you see that man over there? Yesterday, when they served him his lunch they put half a cantaloupe in front of him and thirty minutes later they came to take it away. I stopped the woman removing the tray and I told her, 'This man has had a stroke. He can't eat a cantaloupe like that. You have to scoop it out for him.' So she did scoop it out into bite-sized pieces. Then, the man slowly lowered his spoon, placed one piece upon it at a time, and gently brought them to his mouth. Watching that man eat his cantaloupe yesterday," he concluded, "was one of the finest moments of my life."

No keeping score. No worrying about what he would get in return for his kindness. No excuses. Just finding a way to be kind to another. Just a single decent act. A simple crossing of the line so that others will follow. Tell your loved ones about the good people you have experienced in your life and the times you too have acted with compassion. Lead them now and when you are gone across that line that cuts through the heart of every human being.

CHAPTER 7

What Is Love?

And still, after all this time,
The sun never says to the earth,
"You owe Me."

Look what happens with
A love like that,
It lights the Whole Sky.

—Hafiz

Sometimes I dissolve sugar in a glass bowl in front of young children and ask them to taste the water. "It's sweet," they exclaim as they stick their happily plunged fingers into their giggling mouths.

"Why is it sweet?" I ask, palms up and shoulders shrugged.

"Because you put sugar in it!" they shout.

"Wait a minute. There's sugar in this water?" I say incredulously.

"Yeah, you put it in there. We saw you!" they continue to shout with all their three-year-old might.

"But you can't see the sugar, so how do you know it's there?" I wonder out loud.

Then I direct the whole silly gaggle to the next level of the lesson. "Touch your nose," I say. "Now touch your head. Now your toes, now your ears." They take these directions with glee. "Now listen very carefully," I caution. "Touch the love you feel for your mommy or daddy, brother or sister." The room grows quiet. A few touch their hearts but most are confused. Then I get to tell them about one of the greatest and most beautiful of all truths—that the things we cannot touch or see are nevertheless very real and are called feelings. Feelings, I tell them, are the most important things of all and the most important of all feelings is love.

Later these precious beings will learn that while we cannot see or touch love, we can act with love in what then become life's most real and meaningful moments. Love is the opposite of indifference and of self. The precise moment when Betsy, my wife of thirty-six years, and I met, it was as if the barometric pressure changed all around me. Her blue eyes took my breath away, and they still do. As I mentioned, we became engaged on our second date. Our love was self-evident. It was all feeling and often still is. But it is so much more than that. Love is getting up in the middle of the night to hold her hair back when she's sick and puking in the toilet and then cleaning up after she goes back to bed. Love was when I was suffering from depression after my spinal surgery and too many opioids for too many months. My mood disorder was so bad that if a magic genie had visited me and said, "Steve, I will grant you any wish: world peace, great wealth, an end to all cancer, hunger, oppression, and pain," I would have said, "Leave me alone," and pulled the covers over my head. All I wanted was to be in the dark. On the rare occasions I was hungry, the only thing I felt like eating was Betsy's grilled cheese sandwiches. The kind where she butters and spreads a little mayo on all four sides of the bread, mixes together just the right cheeses, and then grills them to a crispy-outside-and-gooey-inside perfection. During those dark days and weeks and months, Betsy held me, made those comforting sandwiches, carried me to the bathroom, found me the psychological help I had failed to realize I so badly needed, and waited patiently for me to reemerge; all without a hint of complaint or frustration. Love is a selfless, generous thing.

Love makes me want to make Betsy laugh and keep her feet warm at night. Love is the way we worry together about our kids and hold hands under the covers no matter how stressful or argumentative the day. It was emptying her drains after her double mastectomy and assuring her my love was unshakable. It is the way we share sorrow, money, time, tasks, dreams, and failures. It is sex and no sex and the way we do not have to talk when we are together. It is the way she looks in her flannel pajamas when I bring her coffee in bed and the way we look at each other after all these years and say with a grateful sense of arrival, "We're old and married."

Betsy and I are not alone. Every person who feels love knows that it takes a certain magic to begin but a lot of selflessness to grow. Nearly every response to the question of what is love that you will read here contains some element of that selflessness; the placing of another's needs and wants ahead of your own, over and over again. This is true not only of our life partners, but also of parents and children, siblings, family, friends, colleagues, and pets.

Most people think about sacrifice as a loss. We say things like, "It was a terrible sacrifice," or "He made the ultimate sacrifice." But there is an ancient way of thinking about sacrifice that is just the opposite, and I think much closer to the truth. The biblical word for sacrifice is *korban*. Its root meaning is "to draw close or to be near." Sacrifice was the ancients' way of drawing nearer to God. It is also the way we humans draw nearer to each other. Some might say we sacrifice because we love. But the deeper truth is that we love because we sacrifice. To love is to give. It is the most selfless and sacred of things, simple and pure, unseen but felt, and sweet like sugar.

Love is action.

Love is picking up something at the grocery store that you don't like to eat but that your husband adores. Love is dropping everything when your kids call. Love is caring about someone else more than yourself.

At its core, love is about seeing humanity and meaning in others. Love means being at peace with giving more than you take. Love is about sacrifice and surrender of the self to receive connection to others and to the world around you. Love means giving a piece of yourself in order to find a peace in yourself.

Love is that indescribable energy that elevates us to put another person's needs above all others. Love is that force that can take a hatred and dissolve it into forgiveness. Love melts hate and heals the wounds of the soul. Love is freedom from the bondage of self.

⁓

Love is an attitude and a behavior to which you must be committed. If you can feel warm and fuzzy at the same time, good for you! But it's the icing, not the cake. If you don't believe me, think for a minute how incredibly cruel people can be when they claim to love each other.

⁓

Love, as Dr. M. Scott Peck [psychiatrist and author of *The Road Less Traveled*] defines it, is going beyond my own limitations and boundaries to enhance the spiritual growth of myself and others. It is not using the vulnerabilities of others against them and it is a connection to the *Tzelem* [Divine Image] in them.

⁓

Love is the freedom and comfort in knowing that, in good times and bad times, you can be who you are, without judgment.

⁓

Love varies depending on who it is directed to but, overall, it is a feeling of wanting to care for someone else more than yourself. But in addition, my love for my husband, who is deceased, was the butterflies in my stomach when I would see him, the sparkle I saw in his eyes, the feeling that no matter how tough life got, he was the man with whom I wanted to go through the tough times and celebrate the happy times.

For my children, it is the feeling of wanting to protect them from danger and obstacles and hurt all the days of my life with them. It is wanting them to be blessed with a peaceful life.

❧

Love is a feeling of belonging, of feeling just right, of feeling that you are enabled to be your best self and to be better than you are. It is a door that opens in your heart and makes your heart more expansive than it's ever been. It's a feeling of communion, equality, respect, caring, and devotion. It's a feeling of having someone's back and knowing they have yours.

❧

Read 1 Corinthians 13:4–8: "Love is patient. Love is kind. Love is not envious or boastful or arrogant or rude. It does not insist on its own way; it is not irritable or resentful; it does not rejoice in wrongdoing, but rejoices in the truth."

꙳

Love is the courageous act of staying present through the good times and the bad, and never giving up on someone.

꙳

Love shuts down my incessant need to judge and evaluate another. Love is a state of being. Love, if we try to articulate what it means, shrinks.

꙳

I think love is an emotional expression of devotion to another person, to another being (e.g., a pet), to a cause, and to activities in life that make you happy and fulfilled.

꙳

Love for me is the absolute peace and presence I felt when my newborn baby nuzzled her tiny ear by my heart after I fed her.

Present moment. Pure connection.

꙳

It is easier to say what it is not. It is not infatuation, which is focused on the self. It is not entirely altruistic either, since altruism is also focused, to some degree, on the self. Love is focus on the other, even to the detriment of the self, sometimes; and out of love comes devotion, attachment, interdependency, and something more than just self.

~

Ideal love is growing the heart to encompass another without possessing them, to accept and tolerate their foibles without controlling them, to listen with care, to make allowances for differences, to share intimacies with respect and appreciate each other.

~

For me, love means acceptance, and prioritizing someone else's needs above your own, at least some of the time. Love looks different depending on the type of relationship. And it is possible to love someone, but not like them at times (a lesson just about any parent knows well). It can be, in turns, messy, exhilarating, frustrating, and heartbreaking. But any love worth having is ultimately mutual.

~

Love is the special feeling you have for another person that allows you to put them before yourself.

❧

I love this question. Love is covered well by Corinthians, but I'll take us back to my Mayan ancestry where love is defined in a greeting, *ala kesh ala kin*, which means "the light I see in you is the same light in me." I believe the sages of the ages when they say we are all made of love—and that when we connect to this light within ourselves, we are able to see it in each other. Love is vulnerability first and foremost, and it is our humanity, compassion, acceptance, reverence, equity, fairness, and recognition of the beauty and miracles all around us. It's that energy within that lifts even when there's pain or loss. It's that energy that I sometimes feel is God that reminds you inside there is always hope. I feel love in my reverence for nature, for the expanse of the ocean, and the towering mountain peaks that survive the seasons and hundreds of years beyond us.

❧

Love is the nuzzle of your cherished doggy whose nose buries into your knee when you're down. Love is cooking and sharing a great meal and a glass of good wine with friends and family who get you and make you feel you belong. Love is sharing a laugh and a smile that reminds you life is good. Love is allowing that sacred connection, intimacy, sharing, and deep caring—being there for the moments that matter and even those that don't. Love is my child even when she's talking back. Love is life force and the sole reason for being here, I'm sure, if we could just stay ever-present in the light.

❧

Love is unconditional. When you love someone, you accept them for who they are, for better or for worse. Saying you're sorry, even if you're not sure how you really feel. Love is just a feeling—you don't have to think about it—you just feel it. If you have to think about it, it's probably not love.

❧

I learned from my dogs about unconditional love, and particularly our first dog, Lily. Almost every day when I leave for work, Lily stands near the door looking at me, questioning with her eyes if I am going to leave without taking her, and I tell her how hard it is, but I need to leave. When I get home, she runs to me and follows me wherever I go the rest of the night. No conditions, no spite for leaving without her, just love. What a great feeling to be unconditionally loved.

~

What is love?

Consider Rosie, our eighteen-year-old toy poodle who is deaf, blind, and suffering from dementia. Thankfully, she is not in pain. Nevertheless, she confuses day with night and night with day. Betsy and I have to carry her outside to relieve herself several times a day and I am often up with her in the middle of the night while she whimpers for reasons she cannot explain. Rosie has a leaky heart valve that requires medication twice a day and she occasionally bumps her head when she wanders the house. Sometimes she is incontinent. This morning, I held her in my arms as she slept, feeling her tiny heartbeat against my chest. I thought about all the years she has delighted our family, especially when the kids were young. How she intuitively came to me when I was sad or exhausted, and how she refused to leave my side for months the two times in my life I was critically ill. Rosie would love me whether I lived in a mansion or a cardboard box. I mind not at all that she needs me now. Her vulnerability causes me to love her more, not less.

I know I am far from the only pet owner who feels this way about their pet. A crucial difference between our human and animal loved ones is that our animals don't care why we love them, and we couldn't tell them if they did. Whether seldom or often, people say "I love you" to each other, but they almost never say why. The crucial question is: Why not? Now is the time to let the people you love know why. Pour out your gratitude for their sacrifices and yours over the years that have nurtured your love for each other. Tell them how they make you laugh. Tell them what they mean to you and tell them why. Then your love for each other will abide not only for today and tomorrow, but long after you are gone.

CHAPTER 8

Have You Ever Cut Someone Out of Your Life?

You know why salt works on slugs? Because it dissolves in the water that's part of a slug's skin, so the water on the inside of its body starts to flow out. The slug dehydrates. This works with snails, too. And with leeches. And with people like me. With any creature, really, too thin-skinned to stand up for itself.

—Jodi Picoult

I was surprised by the number of people who reached out to me about a particular paragraph in my last book. They thanked me for telling the truth about something that most people don't talk about. It is something I learned in my own life and over many years of helping to quell the fears of others. The fear addressed in that paragraph that attracted so much attention arises more often than most people know. It is the anticipation of guilt imagining what it will feel like when someone with whom you have cut off contact dies. The conversations go something like this. "I haven't spoken to my mother in years. She has been cold and withholding my entire life. Every time I was with her as an adult and often as a child I ended up feeling awful about myself and frustrated with her inability to listen to me and respect who I am. But now that she is dying I am afraid I am going to regret not making peace with her."

"I doubt it," is my honest response. "You will most likely feel relieved." People are often surprised to hear this, but the truth is that if a person constantly hurt and disappointed you while living, the odds are that person will continue to hurt and disappoint you while dying. Dying doesn't generally give anyone a new personality. Not you. Not her. Not most people.

My own mother didn't speak to her father for more than forty years. He was a part of my childhood one day, and gone the next. She never shared the precise reason she cut him out of her life and mine. All she said was, "He's a mean, ignorant man." I later learned that she watched as he beat her brothers when she and they were young and that my grandmother struggled with mental illness, eventually dying by suicide when I was a little boy. It seemed everything about her father caused my mother pain. One day, likely with my father's help, she stood up for herself and banished him from her life. When I was younger,

I thought her decision set a terrible example for me and my four siblings. Isn't "family first" the way it's supposed to be?

More than thirty years after last seeing my grandfather I decided to seek him out. I had recently given a sermon about the importance of taking care of our unfinished emotional business and realized I ought to take my own advice. My grandfather lived in the same little house in Minneapolis where I had last seen him decades before. I wrote to him, got his phone number, and visited. It didn't take long for me to realize that my mother was right. It was clear to me that, long ago, she either had to protect herself or be demeaned and possibly emotionally destroyed by her father.

I am not suggesting that we stop trying to maintain relationships with people who can sometimes be difficult or annoying. There wouldn't be a married couple on earth if that were the case. I am talking about something more rare and extreme, which is a person who is toxic to your well-being. You might wonder why I included a question like this as something to consider sharing with the people you love. The reason is that it speaks to a much larger and important lesson, which is that there are times when we courageously and sometimes painfully have to stand up for ourselves.

This has been a very difficult thing for me to do because of the way in which my personal and professional lives are so intertwined. In most cases, to end a relationship with someone who has disrespected or hurt me is to simultaneously disengage with someone who is also a member of my congregation that I am obligated to serve and care for. Besides, clergy are supposed to be slow to anger, quick to forgive, and understanding and empathetic with people who behave badly because they have almost surely been emotionally wounded. Add to that the reality that most clergy choose their path partly because we want to be liked and, to top it off, we know full well refusing to engage with too many people (or even a single person with power and wealth) can mean the end of our tenure in the congregation. Most people have been kind, grateful, and respectful throughout my career. A few have gossiped or lied about me to others, been unfairly judgmental and even cruel. To put it bluntly, as clergy you either eat shit or risk the consequences of standing up for yourself. I have done both. The older I get, the less willing I am to put up with people who are unkind. I am getting better at standing up for myself. It's a lesson I wish I had learned sooner.

I found some people, besides myself, who were willing to talk about their experiences cutting off, letting go, or walking away from relationships that weren't good for them. May we all learn from each other.

❧

Ah, this is painful. There's a difference between never giving up on anyone and allowing someone to do their worst without complaint. So yes, there are people who've had to be uninvited to my life. It is so critical to be honest with yourself—are you hurt by this person because they bring something up in you that you don't want to look at? That's not a reason to cut them out of your life. But there are people who are working out their own confusion, and it is a big mistake to think that you're doing them or yourself any favors by not shutting the door and moving on. Are we staying because of people-pleasing or thinking that we are someone's last hope? That's just ego-centered and not truly benefiting anyone. No, some of my most dramatic growth has come from those times that I have spoken, clearly and boldly, "You shall not pass" (and anyone who truly knows me knows that's a reference to Gandalf in *The Fellowship of the Ring*).

I have had to cut people out of my life because they were bad for my sense of being and appealed to the lowest, basest part of me. Seeing each person for who they are, not who you need them to be, is the key to avoiding people who are not good for you. They may be good people, they just aren't good for you.

Sometimes goodbye is a gift—to you and to them. I believe that people come into our lives for a reason, a season, or a lifetime. Separation is never easy, but sometimes it is necessary. When my relationship with a particular person ceases to make me a better person, it's time to move on.

I've never had a relationship so toxic that I've had to cut the cord, but I have on occasion let the cord stretch so far that it has almost snapped. Rarely is it about the person. It's about the circumstances. We don't like to believe that relationships are context-dependent, but they are, unless you and the other person make a huge effort to lift the relationship above the situational level. It is so energy- and time-consuming that you can't do it that often. In a nutshell, this is why marriage is so challenging. No matter what else is happening, you must always prioritize the relationship.

I've been cut out more than I've cut someone off. In all cases, when it was a romantic breakup, I got sympathy and support. The one case when a friend cut me out was more difficult to grasp and accept, and I received little to no support. Friends drop us by drifting away all the time, until we get the hint. But I got a "Dear Janet" letter from a very dear platonic male friend. I was poison to him; he wasn't getting what he really wanted. His leaving was wise and self-protective.

I think when it comes to romantic partners, there should be a "three strikes and you're out" rule. We often find ourselves entangled in relationships that just aren't constructive to one or both partners. When you care about that person, give it three tries to convert to positive dynamics—with guidance counseling if you both really want it to work—then bite the bullet and let go. Life's too short to drag out relationships that will never be healthy. Insofar as I value platonic friends just as highly as romantic ones, I suppose the same rule would apply.

❦

I had to end a friendship with a longtime female friend from college when I heard she had been bad-mouthing me behind my back and also started dating an old boyfriend of mine. I knew that even if I forgave her, I couldn't trust her again to have my best interests at heart. I did it in the form of a letter, which I would not advise. (This was before email and texting.) I didn't give her a chance to defend herself. Not that it would have changed my mind, but it would have been fairer. I would tell my loved ones that if there is someone they need to cut out of their lives, they should think about what they want to say. Practice saying it. Then talk to the person over the phone or do it face-to-face. Ghosting them is a cop-out. Texting them is rude. Honest, clear, and calm communication is always the best.

❧

I'm friends with almost all of my exes. There is no family member I won't talk to. There are times when people struggling need to have hard guardrails to get them back on track, but beyond a momentary withdrawal from interacting with folks, I have always either come back to them or let them know I am here to come back to. Even with some of my so-called worst enemies, I keep a line open and hope warming like old but steady coals.

❧

I did have to cut a best friend out of my life. We met young and as we grew, we changed. Just because you end a relationship doesn't mean you have to hate them or wish them ill will. Send them off in peace and love.

❧

When our son was divorced, his ex wished to maintain a relationship with my wife and me. Given the facts that surrounded the breakup, we felt a fundamental behavioral line had been crossed, and, much as we had had a fine relationship with her, the crossing of that line could not be ignored; the affront to our family and its values was simply too great.

❧

Yes, and I almost would add, "of course." When it happens, rather than the usual drifting away that characterizes the departure of friends, it is because there was something injurious and dangerous about the relationship. In the end, if someone wants to disrupt the protective structures that get us through the day, you have to decide whether the intent is therapeutic or just antagonistic. And therapeutic disruption is best accomplished by therapists, or not at all!

❧

My husband was the hardest goodbye, not because I didn't love him—I did. It was hard because I knew to live the life I longed to live, it would have to be without him.

I have made other hard choices with friends who no longer fit into my world. My daughter has had similar challenges and we have spoken about the crossroads we come to when we feel it's time to say goodbye. It doesn't have to be angry or ugly, it just has to come from being clear with your convictions, values, and sense of being. When you no longer feel good, healthy, positive, accepted, or trusting in a relationship and you have done all you can, it is okay to walk away.

I use this line a lot: "Be willing to betray others' expectations of you to be true to yourself."

~

A close friend of mine betrayed me in a business setting, letting others accuse me of doing something I would never do. I was so incredibly hurt, but because of our long-term relationship I justified her actions to myself and others. My husband helped me to finally stand up for myself and realize that our friendship had a pattern of unhealthy behaviors. I decided to cut off the relationship. When I did, I could breathe better, my body was more relaxed, and I felt stronger about using my voice. I tell this story often to my daughters because I want them to know that it is always important to live with integrity and stand up for yourself.

I do have one friendship that had to be cut off. This was during a time when I was younger, before I had children, and this friend and her then-boyfriend played a very central role in the life of my household. Truthfully, it was painful to lose their presence in my life, but I understood that the relationship wasn't particularly balanced and healthy. I would hope to impart to my family the idea that all relationships shift and change over time, and where we're able to shift and grow with someone a relationship can last and deepen. But also— sometimes a relationship is unhealthy or toxic, and it's okay to let it go.

I definitely had to move away from certain people in my life, and sadly some of them are my family. What I learned is that unfortunately there are some relationships that cannot survive and it's okay. I believe it doesn't make you or the other person a bad person. It just ends up this way sometimes.

The lesson is don't give up too easily—try as hard as you can to make the relationship work—but at some point, when it's time to move on, move on, and don't beat yourself up. Continue to wish good things upon your estranged loved ones and do not speak ill of them.

❧

Hopefully, when we make a mistake, we can accept responsibility for it, apologize, and make amends. In doing so, we hopefully attract the same type of person in our relationships. But sometimes we will have those in our life that are not kind, that use us or betray us. When someone shows you that they are that person, let them go.

❧

Do not hold a grudge. Move on and understand why it is important to not have that person in your life.

❧

Did you ever have to cut someone out of your life? What lesson is there within that decision to guide your loved ones in their relationships?

My friend Rich's aunt was the only immediate family member to survive the Second World War, along with Rich's father. This aunt, with looks and cunning, saved herself and her brother but never let him forget it. She did everything in her power to control him, telling him he wasn't smart enough to be successful, which he sadly came to believe. She was belittling and cruel to Rich's mother too.

For Rich, the moment of truth came when his father called her one day to brag about Rich's older brother Isaac's academic achievements. Isaac was a brilliant thirteen-year-old. The aunt's response was to say that it was too bad Rich would never amount to anything. Rich remembers his mother was listening in on the call and suddenly started screaming at his aunt, but he was six years old and thought maybe his aunt was right. Maybe his brother did get all the brains in the family and Rich was destined to be the same failure his aunt claimed his father was.

Despite his mother telling him there were no limits to what he could achieve in his life, that insecure six-year-old boy, already embarrassed because he had to wear bifocals, wasn't so sure. But somehow he decided that he wouldn't speak to his aunt again and would do everything he could to prove her wrong. "One of my greatest pleasures in life is that my aunt lived to see my success," he told me nearly sixty years later. "Maybe the most important lesson I can teach my kids is you do not let anyone in your life keep you down. There are too many people who will make you feel good about yourself, so there is no need to keep people around that suck the life out of you, who have little good to say about anyone so they can feel better about themselves. No one needs negative energy in their life."

We each have a line that once crossed by another creates damage that cannot be undone or excused. Physical abuse; a breach of trust by telling an embarrassing, painful secret to others; an outright lie to or about us; always taking, never giving; ghosting; gossiping—whatever your line is, at some point someone close to you will likely cross it and you will have to make a decision. There is a lot for your loved ones to learn from those moments. Tell them your "when I had to cut someone out of my life to stand up for myself" story. Because as much as we all want to be respected by others, it's self-respect that matters most.

CHAPTER 9

How Do You Want to Be Remembered?

Think about a good memory, she whispers in my mind.
Remember a moment when you loved him.
And just like that, I do.

—Cynthia Hand

I play a sort of visual regression game in my head when I meet old people. I learned this technique many years ago from a hospital chaplain. He told me that when visiting the elderly in the hospital or nursing home, a lot of people unwittingly make the mistake of treating them like children. They speak loudly and slowly, avoid complex issues and emotions, keep it short, and leave. "What I do to check myself," he told me, "is as soon as I walk in the room, I look carefully at the person's face and then try to imagine what they looked like when they were thirty or forty years younger. Then, I relate to them as if they are that younger age. It's important to remember that everyone was younger once—more vibrant, happy, in love, having fun, and full of dreams. Someone might be elderly, but there is still a lot of that younger person inside. Respect and relate to that person as much as you can."

I have taken his advice for more than thirty years, and not just in hospitals and nursing homes. I play the same game standing in line at the grocery store as I watch an old woman in her motorized scooter with a basket in front. She is taking a long time to check out with coupons and questions, trying my patience. So I imagine her at her wedding, robed in white lace. She is in her early twenties, beautiful, with a shy smile and chestnut eyes. Her man is home from the war. She is wearing bright red lipstick, her eyebrows are thick, dark, and perfectly shaped, and her curly jet-black hair is topped with a tulle veil. Above the V-shaped neckline a single strand of simple pearls adorns her neck. I watch her feeding a first slice of cake to her handsome new husband as flashbulbs pop, and then, they dance. She twirls, happy, laughing, and dizzy. They have an irrepressible urge for life and love. "Next," the cashier says, snapping me out of my fantasy as the old woman motors away toward the automatic exit door.

My father suffered from Alzheimer's for ten years. At first it aged him; eventually it turned him into a different person. In a way he died twice. First, when the disease changed his brain and therefore him into someone who was no longer my dad and to whom I was no longer a son. Years later he died again when his heart stopped beating and he passed quietly in the middle of the night, like a breeze. I was two thousand miles away.

Each time I visited my dad in the nursing home I would bend down to his level in his wheelchair, lean over cheek to cheek, and ask someone to take a picture of us. I have dozens of those photos on my phone. I wanted each one in case it would end up being the last picture from the last time I ever saw my dad alive. It seemed right at the time and I can't bring myself to delete them, but I hate those photos now of me smiling to disguise a breaking heart and him slack-jawed and staring into space. They are not how I want to remember my father. They are how I want to forget him. Now, more than four years since his death, I swipe to other pictures of him far more often. One my sister sent to me last year, circa 1980. My dad is on roller skates alongside his best friend Joey, gliding around the rink with a wide smile, free and relaxed. He was having fun. My mom must have been taking a break with Joey's wife, Nancy, when she snapped that one. There is another of him seated in front of a sundae with three extra pitchers of divine, liquefied hot fudge in front of him. He's wearing his baggy red flannel shirt with a slightly used napkin in the pocket, spoon halfway to his mouth and a drip of hot fudge on his chin just below his wide, beautiful smile and sparkling blue eyes. "Where are you, Dad?" I ask out loud in the quiet privacy of my home office as I gaze at those images from happier times. "Where are you?"

I know the answer to my own question. He is in my mind because of the most extraordinary gift bestowed upon human beings—memory. Unlike any other creature on earth we have the ability to summon the past into the present and carry it with us into the future. We can envision the people we love before the dementia, the tumor, the doctors, the needles, and the tubes; before the funeral and the turning of the spade; before the crushing weight of early grief and the mercifully gentler ebb and flow of loss for a lifetime. Memory painfully causes us to revisit the past; the decline of someone we deeply loved. But memory also enables us to transcend that pain to remember our loved ones in their finest, most content, fulfilled, and happy moments. What memories of you do you wish for your loved ones to carry? What images will dance in their hearts like a bride twirling in the perfumed air, happy and alive?

~

I am hiking among tall redwood trees, wearing jeans and a sweatshirt. I am fifty years old, with my dog. My parents and grandparents and aunts and uncles are waiting for me at the bottom of the trail. They can't wait to hug me.

~

I would just hope you see me happy and smiling. Maybe I am on the beach, it's a warm day, and I'm in a long, flowy white dress. I am with Elvis.

I went to meet our youngest granddaughter's new puppy recently. I rolled on the ground with that puppy. He slobbered all over me, amidst roars of laughter. They have seen me so often around the Shabbat table. They have seen me lecture and preach and teach. They have witnessed the love and the acts of love which bind me and their grandmother together.

My older grandchildren study with me. Let them remember my rumpled, unkempt Zoom appearances. Many of the kids have gone boogie boarding with me—and I was in a black wetsuit. Remember that. I have changed their diapers. They have witnessed my illness and aging. I want to be remembered in all of my complexity—because that's who I am.

My wife, my sons, my very best friends, will, I suspect, see me in ways unique to my relationship with them. I do not have anything I "want" them to see. I hope they will see what was important to each one of them. It would be even better if they talked amongst themselves about these things.

I would have Amy imagining me at Jazz Fest in New Orleans, wearing a T-shirt and shades, taking a bite out of a fried oyster po'boy while listening to some great music. I'm probably in my forties.

I want my loved ones to envision a kind and gentle person whom others called a mensch. I would want to be thought of at home, on vacation with my family, and with my friends enjoying each other's company. Also, doing things with my wife such as simply watching TV together, traveling together, and just enjoying each other's company. I would rather be dressed casually than formally. I would love to be pictured with my wife and daughters enjoying being together.

This is an easy one! This could be today! I want them to see . . . Me with Bob, he's smiling with me, we're with a group of our friends, I'm dressed to the nines, maybe even wearing a hat(!), certainly flashing lots of the fabulous jewelry Bob's given me over the years. It's spring and the garden is bursting, we're all under the olive trees, and our three golden retrievers are with us! Heaven!

❧

I would like them to see me reading and learning. I would like them to remember that I always wanted to learn new things and that I always wanted to share my knowledge of the world with them.

I am probably wearing either jeans or sweatpants and a white T-shirt. I would be well over a hundred at this time.

And I hope that at each holiday they celebrate, they will remember how important I felt it was to gather family and friends for holidays and special events.

❧

Well, I'm one of the few answering these questions who already has been to the World to Come when my heart stopped beating for several minutes, and it's not so bad! No white light, no escorts taking my soul to the netherworld. I therefore don't think about it. When I counsel patients, I tell them that it is certainly much easier to get on that train than to be left at the station. Leaving ought not to be painful, if your soul has accomplished what it was intended on this Earth to do.

~

I think I'd like them to envision me with my grandmother, mom, and best friend, enjoying live musical theater somewhere. Or possibly in the kitchen baking, but not for business, just for fun. Either way I'm listening to or watching a musical, and in a happy place.

~

For seventeen days in summer 2012 at the London Olympics we were truly a family. I want my family to envision the joy of that trip. When we all got along and moved in the same direction. Everyone accommodated the other. That was our first major trip as a family, with just our family. Every day was planned to a point, but we accommodated different family members' requests, and everyone was excited to see a different event. My daughter loved gymnastics, my wife loved track and field, and my son loved swimming. I loved seeing them enjoy my sixth Olympics and their first.

I want them to see how happy we all were together. Limited fighting or jockeying for position, but just being a family. I just want to see us as a family. It doesn't get better than that and nothing else matters.

Ahhhh, I am free of the flesh suit, I am ageless and forever, I am with everyone and no one, I am part of the current of God's grid, alive in a way I can sense but have never known. I want my loved ones to feel that love energy alive within them always. I want them to see me in the dancing sun glittering in the leaves of big giant oak trees with a glorious backdrop of snowcapped mountains and cascading waterfalls showering mist into the valleys. I am a part of that energy in nature that lives, breathes, dances, and inspires awe just at the sight of such beauty. I am with the energy of my doggies playing with Frisbees and chasing balls. I am free and a part of all life force and ever present in every breath you take, in every beautiful encounter, in every lick of a dog, in every smile, and in every expression of art—I want you to feel me home and a part of the grandeur that has no end. I don't envision myself in flesh form, with people who have passed. I sense a calling to be home with all the energies of love I've known back into the big sea where we all swim as one. I hope my loved ones see me in nature, free, expansive, and ever present in my lasting love.

I am wearing sweats and enjoying a beautiful meal with my late husband.

I want them only to remember what makes them happy, whatever small or big moments we shared together that made them feel good. I do not need them remembering my greatness or my accomplishments; I want them to feel the private feelings we shared. I am not fearful of people forgetting what I did; I want to make sure they are able to feel how we made each other feel. There will be no one left who really remembers me as a baby, few who will distinctly remember me as a child, so I hope that they will remember me as I came to this life and this time on earth. And maybe I'm unshaved, casual, but carrying a really nice smile that lights up their day.

I think it would have to be me in my fifties, climbing the rocky, treacherous trails of Kauai, with my husband and daughter, in hiking gear, muddy shoes, scrapes and bruises galore from stumbling, salt water in my hair, and a huge grin on my face even as I thought I might pass out from exhaustion.

Just remember me at my best. Laughing, smiling, listening to the music I love. And passionately engaged in my work and witness to love and serve others.

When I'm gone, I hope my loved ones will keep my memory alive by telling funny stories about me and remember how much I loved each and every one of them. I hope when they're outside and they see a beautiful flower or bird, even a lizard, they'll remember how I used to speak to those flowers, birds, and lizards. Maybe they'll even do that themselves. I hope if they like they will keep a picture or two of me around and talk to me. I promise if they listen carefully, I will answer.

I'd like them to see me returning home from a walk in my Lululemons and sweatshirt, pink cheeks from the fresh air, twinkle in my eyes, and a smile on my face. I'm whatever age they loved me at the best. I'm with my husband and all three of our kids, possibly their partners and a couple of grandchildren would be nice. Just sitting in the backyard, hanging out in the sunshine. Laughing and loving each other.

~

I want my loved ones to see my smile, my heart, and my love for them and humankind. I will be the one with the sign that says, "Everything is possible with God." I will be with all of my deceased relatives, my father, mother, aunts and uncles, cousins, and my brother as well as my friends and teachers. I will be in the air they breathe and as close as their call.

~

They won't be able to tell what age I am because I will be wrapped to the eyeballs in a black down coat, standing on a sheet of ice, at dusk, waiting to see an owl fly out.

~

When your loved ones want to envision you after you die, what do you want them to see? Where are you? How old are you? Who are you with? What are you wearing? What are you doing?

There is yet another blessing given to human beings. We not only have the ability to remember, but we also have the ability to consciously create memories for others to hold. I often say to my children when we are in the midst of some excellent moment, "Remember me this way. Tell your children about it." Sometimes they roll their eyes and tell me to stop being so "lifey." But mostly, they listen and quietly take a mental picture to summon at will decades from now. They know my advice to capture a moment isn't just that of their father, but of someone who has heard a thousand families share their memories a day before a loved one's funeral; someone who knows what sticks in the mind and lives in the heart long after we are gone and that we never really know when that day will be.

You can decide while you are alive which memories and moments you want to create for your loved ones to hold; what beauty for them to embrace when the sadness of loss creeps into their hearts. Help them see you as you yourself want to be seen, to remember you as you wish to be remembered, to feel your love for them when only memory and love remain.

CHAPTER 10

What Is Good Advice?

Good advice is rarer than rubies.

—Salman Rushdie

The Lebanese American writer and artist Kahlil Gibran was right when he said, "In one drop of water are found all the secrets of all the oceans; in one aspect of you are found all the aspects of existence." While I consider it a gift, my wife and kids often tease me about my inclination to summarize a complex problem or solution with a single saying. I can't help it. I was raised in a household where Yiddish expressions were the primary vehicle for teaching life lessons. I then went on to study ancient texts that often distill a lengthy argument between schools of scholars over centuries down to a single, briefly worded teaching. I have also learned over the years that many of the most important things we ever say require only a few words. "Yes. No. I do. It's a girl! He's gone. Guilty. I love you. I'm sorry. It's okay. I'm here." We can say so much with merely a word or two or three. Aphorisms, expressions, proverbs, and slogans are crystalized wisdom to guide the people we love in life and long after with just a few simple and vitally important words.

Some expressions are wise, some are funny, and many are both. My brother and I were going to write and deliver our father's eulogy using nothing but his favorite expressions he repeated endlessly to teach us finance, street smarts, respect, and perspective on our own problems. Here are a few:

For perspective on our problems: "Whatever it is, it's better than a boil on your ass."

On the pain of poverty: "When a poor bride gets up to dance, the band takes a leak."

On saving money: "A little is a lot."

On setting priorities: "You can't sit on two chairs with one *tuchus*."

On how life can be unfair: "'Balls,' said the queen, 'If I had them I'd be king.'"

On respect: "The boss isn't always right, but he's still the boss."

On perseverance: "If you push, it goes" (double entendre intended).

On doctors and auto mechanics: "If they look, they find."

On being dealt a bad hand: "It is what it is."

On seeing beneath the surface of a person: "You can put earrings on a pig, but it's still a pig."

For my father, these expressions had value of biblical proportions. They were his gospel, his teaching, his warnings, his guidance, his legacy distilled that he wanted to bequeath to his children so we would not lose our way when he was gone. So that we could continue to hear his voice, feel his presence, protecting us and guiding us at life's crossroads. He was right. He died years ago and yet, when I am faced with a decision or asked for advice by others, I often lean on his simple, sometimes funny, sometimes crude, but always spot-on expressions. It's one of the most meaningful ways he lives on.

What a treasure trove of sayings people gave me when I asked! What a joy to gather them here to share with you. This chapter is going to be fun to read and useful too. Enjoy!

This one by Emperor Augustus is one my brother uses and that I repeat to myself and often to friends seeking advice: "Make haste slowly."

I also use "Ain't over till the fat lady sings"—I think of my friend's mom, widowed in her fifties, who entered a second marriage at age ninety. You really never know your story until it's over.

Sometimes less is more.
Just because you think you know the answer, don't stop
    thinking about the problem.
If you save a life, you can save the world.
Above all, do no harm.
Think before you speak.

Secondary characters are main characters in their own
    lives.
It's not the mistake that defines you, it's how you behave
    afterward.
Love your planet. It's the only one you've got.
"You're my little chu-chi face." (This is a line

from a song in *Chitty Chitty Bang Bang*, describing
how I feel about my kids when I want to squeeze
them.)

Judaism is a garden that's been growing for four
thousand years. Are you really going to let it die on
your watch?

~

Dear God, relieve me of the bondage of self.

Do you prefer to be right, or do you prefer to be happy?

When you pray, be prepared to be divinely
inconvenienced.

My disease wants me dead, but it'll settle for miserable!

~

"Your task is not to seek for love, but merely to seek and
find all the barriers within yourself that have built
against it." —RUMI

"Make good trouble." —JOHN LEWIS

"Don't go to the hardware store for milk."
    —AUTHOR UNKNOWN

"Everyone you meet is fighting a battle you know
nothing about. Be kind. Always." —ROBIN WILLIAMS

"Pick your battles. You don't have to show up to every
argument you're invited to." —MANDY HALE

"What is it you plan to do with your one wild and
   precious life?" —MARY OLIVER

Look for the ordinary magic in every day.
Success is getting up just one more time than you fall.
May all beings be happy and free from fear and harm.

Just the other day I heard an old man use the expression
allen jüdische kinder gesagt, which literally means "all
Jewish children say." It is intended to put your problem
in proper perspective, as in "Anyone able to say this is
fortunate," or "Everyone should have such problems." I
said to him, "Where'd you ever hear that? My grandma
used that all the time when we complained about our
losses, or our pampered sufferings." He answered that
he used to work as a teenager in the kosher Jewish hotels
of the Catskills, and he heard all the old-time
expressions. It made me smile. We have so much, that
most of our little failures and our foibles would be
considered riches sufficient for our brethren and we
should be grateful for them, even for the losses. Some of
the other Viennese Jewish old-time expressions my
grandmother used to use when we broke something or

did something wrong: "*Malheur* [French for "catastrophe"], I've lost much more than that." And finally, the one that her own mom used to use when talking about my father was that Dad had a *bittere gevureh*, a strength informed by bitter suffering in life.

❧

Pain is essential, suffering is optional.

Repent each day and fail forward.

If there is this much shit, there must be a pony here someplace.

What am I going to learn today?

Do the next right thing, no matter how you feel.

❧

Be fearless.

Stay humble.

Learn to listen (and to hear).

Lead with love.

Take life's work seriously, but don't take life too seriously.

❧

You are what your deepest desire is

As is your desire, so is your intent

As is your intent, so is your will
As is your will, so is your deed
As is your deed, so is your destiny.

From the Upanishads. Each line gave me clarity and a path for living with intent.

～

Be yourself.
Be authentic.
Be kind.
Try to be a person that people enjoy being around.
Always learn and grow.

～

If it's that important, they'll call back.
Be confident; it makes it easier for other people.
Don't skip to the end.
Love means always having to say you're sorry.
"We're on to Cincinnati." —COACH BILL BELICHICK

～

In the Bible, Jonathan wept over the departure of his
closest friend, King David, but the king decided that
action was more important than weeping.
People can suck. Get over it.

I really love you and I trust you. I really do.

"Teach them diligently unto your children."

—DEUTERONOMY 6:7

You are one of a kind. Never forget that.

❧

"Always stay humble and kind." —TIM MCGRAW

"If you can't say something nice, don't say nothing at all."

—THUMPER FROM *BAMBI*

"When someone shows you who they are, believe them the first time." —MAYA ANGELOU

❧

How do you eat an elephant? One bite at a time.

You don't ask, you don't get.

No rain, no rainbow.

State the obvious.

"If I am not for myself, who will be for me? If I am only for myself, what am I? And if not now, when?"

—RABBI HILLEL THE ELDER

❧

Start your day with a positive thought.

End your day in prayer counting your blessings.

Make yourself as big as you can.

Be grateful that you can move your body.

A smile is the best thing you can put on your face.

❧

You have to do what you have to do.

If you are going to do it, do it, and do not look back.

If she dies, she dies. (There are some things out of your
control that you are just going to have to accept.)

Does it get any better than this?

No tree grows to heaven.

❧

There is no rebate for selling your soul.

You can do anything, but you cannot do everything.

Don't major in the minors.

Some of you is not the sum of you.

If you fall, fall fighting.

❧

"I've learned that people will forget what you said,
people will forget what you did, but people
will never forget how you made them feel."
—MAYA ANGELOU

"I'm just a girl who cain't say no, cain't seem to
say it at all." —ADO ANNIE, *OKLAHOMA!*

"Make new friends, but keep the old. One is silver and the other gold." —JOSEPH PARRY, VIA THE GIRL SCOUTS

❧

I am you.

Where there is a will, there is a way.

Believe.

You reap what you sow.

We are enough.

❧

"Never, never, never quit." —WINSTON CHURCHILL

"Pick yourself up, dust yourself off and start all over again." —FROM THE FILM *SWING TIME*

This too shall pass.

Enjoy yourself; it's later than you think!

❧

You pick your friends, and not your family, so pick wisely.

The shortest distance between two points is a straight line. Or, said differently, why make something complicated when you can make it simple?

You cannot beat genetics. (My kids have definitely taught me that, which I always suspected.)

If something starts fucked up it usually ends fucked up.

(The first rule of bankruptcy law.)

If three people know a secret, two better be dead.

(I borrowed that from Ben Franklin and have learned in life that few people are capable of keeping confidences.)

❧

What are your top five sayings that encapsulate the accrued wisdom of your life experience?

"You know what Mom would say right now?" is something I hear a lot when I am gathered with a family before a funeral to talk about their loved one who has died. What follows more often than not is one of Mom's, or Dad's, or Papa's, or Grandma's favorite sayings, which served as a guide to the people they loved while alive, is helping them still through the sadness, and will remain with those loved ones for the rest of their lives. You can advise your loved ones for as long as they live with just a few simple words: words that carry important truths, words that will make them smile and laugh, words that will make them think and protect them from pain. Tell them now. Hand them wisdom compact enough to carry with them now and always.

CHAPTER 11

What Will Your Epitaph Say?

Live your epitaph.

—Zoe Weil

When politicians, celebrities, and even ordinary people profess one set of values and are then discovered to be living their lives by a very different set of values, it often leads to an embarrassing downfall. Social media and the "gotcha" ethos of our culture mean there is very little forgiveness for those who are revealed to be phonies. It is also very difficult and emotionally painful to lead that kind of double life. The anxiety and the cognitive dissonance can be unbearable. A lot of people who are "outed" in some way will tell you how liberating it is to finally stop living disingenuously. Consider former Speaker of the House Jim Wright, who was caught committing sixty-nine ethics violations and forced to resign in disgrace. Once his secret was out and he started living in alignment with what he knew was right, he said, "I am so much better off physically, financially, mentally, and in almost every other way."

Most of us feel like an imposter at some point because we are not really who others believe we are. Every clergyperson I know is waiting for the fraud squad to show up and expose the fact that none of us feel we are fully living up to the demands and standards of our calling. Every parent realizes early on that their child sees them as bigger than life, wiser and stronger than is humanly possible. My more than three decades of listening to people confess their shortcomings has taught me that we all have a secret we don't want anyone else to discover. We are all ashamed of something. That's actually a normal part of what it means to be human.

But when who you present yourself to be is in profound and near constant contrast to how you actually live, there is likely great pain ahead for you. The calmest, happiest, most at-peace people I know are those who strive and succeed at closely aligning their behavior with their beliefs. That is why this question of your epitaph is so vitally important not only when you die. Whether or not you plan to have a grave or headstone, you can use the constraints they require to clarify your purpose: distilling the essence of your life down to four lines with no more than fifteen characters per line, you engage in a powerful form of essentialism. Your epitaph will leave an important message for others after you die. But more important, choosing those words now and sharing them with those who will read them literally or figuratively carved in stone when you are gone is an opportunity to think deeply about your most cherished values and whether or not you are living up to those values. For most of us, the answer is sometimes. For others the answer is an honest and painful no.

It's never too late to be the person you aspire to be. My Muslim friend and community leader put it this way: "As important as prayer has been in my life, there have been times when I have walked away from it out of shame because I did something that was out of alignment with my values, feeling sinful and unworthy of God's love. But reminders of God's infinite grace, mercy, and love have helped me come back to prayer. When holding strong self-judgment, I go to these words of Rumi that give me solace: 'Come, come, whoever you are. Wanderer, worshiper, lover of leaving. It doesn't matter. Ours is not a caravan of despair. Come, even if you have broken your vows a thousand times. Come, yet again, come, come.'"

The British rabbi Sylvia Rothschild tells a story, via Martin Buber, of the great Hasidic rabbi Zusya of Hanipol:

On his deathbed he began to cry uncontrollably and his students and disciples tried hard to comfort him. They asked him, "Rabbi, why do you weep? You are almost as wise as Moses, you are almost as hospitable as Abraham, and surely heaven will judge you favourably."

Zusya answered them: "It is true. When I get to heaven, I won't worry so much if God asks me, 'Zusya, why were you not more like Abraham?' or 'Zusya, why were you not more like Moses?' I know I would be able to answer these questions. After all, I was not given the righteousness of Abraham or the faith of Moses but I tried to be both hospitable and thoughtful. But what will I say when God asks me, 'Zusya, why were you not more like Zusya?'"

We are all merely human. We stumble and fall, stumble and fall. We become distracted and seduced by shiny, empty things. We lose our way. We crawl sometimes, burdened with shame, until we find the strength to rise up and walk a more righteous, loving path. Most people think of a headstone as something for others when we are no more, which of course it is. But this opportunity to choose while alive what will truly be your final words when you are gone is a challenge to examine your life and ask, "Are you truly being you?"

I would like my headstone to be a eucalyptus tree. Its medicinal properties will live on well beyond me. I want to provide shade and relief for others long after I am gone. To have a place for my loved ones to meditate and breathe more intentionally. If they decide to have a headstone or some kind of marker, I would like it to say, "Sit with the silence of love."

~

Love connects us all. When we are loved, we become our better selves. When we overlook one another's faults and help each other, we grow together and nurture each other. Returning to the source of God's love can transform the harshest of our circumstances. You are not alone. God's very breath and mercy are always with you.

~

*Eshet Hayil** mom wife sister
aunt daughter niece
cousin friend

I realize that I am who I am in relation to the people around me. Besides being a mother and wife, I'm defined by my devotion to others in my family. When it comes to holidays and celebrations and milestones, I'm the center of the family. I'm an attentive daughter to my

---

* *Eshet Hayil* means "a woman of valor."

parents, involved aunt, loving sister, sharing niece, supportive cousin, and loyal and fun friend. But mostly, I feel that I am a woman of valor. I try to live a moral life and be a good role model to my kids and husband.

Smile
Find Your Joy
Give Thanks
Or: I can't even fit a full tweet on this thing?!?

A full life
Well-lived
Open heart and mind
On to the next one!

He was a mensch.

He loved and served his people.

Made us laugh.

No headstone for me.

Husband. Father. Grandfather.
How great are God's works.

Devoted mom and wife who always tried her best.

It is hard being a parent and especially alone. All I can do is to try my best and I hope that someday they will understand.

Hineni—Here I am

Richard Loved His Family Deeply
and Made Everyone Around Him Better

The first part of my headstone reflects the obvious: I deeply love my family. I want people for generations to know that. The second part of my headstone is to reflect my ultimate goal in life: to make people around me better people, which is what I believe all of us should strive to do. I still have a ways to go before accomplishing both parts of my headstone, but I will do the best I can until the day I die.

❧

Loving mother & friend

Because nothing else matters.

❧

Things may not
Be what they
Seem, but
Persist anyway.

❧

Loving husband and father.
A great healer and mensch.
He enjoyed life.

❧

He was warm and loving.
He took care of people.
He imparted wisdom.
He spoke truth.

I won't write it for them. I had to spend a lot of time
writing three of them already, so I'm not going to make
it that easy! But they will need to find some biblical verse
that communicates that I somehow redeemed the
suffering of the ones who came before me, as much as
man can do so.

Questions I asked:
Who am I?
What do I want?
How can I serve?

Wife and mother
Daughter and friend
Baker and laugher!
Community builder

I had this written on my husband's headstone: "Later is
now."

It meant that whenever I asked him something he didn't want to talk about, he would say, "Not now, later!" I have written my headstone and it will say: "In the end, together again."

~

What will your epitaph say? A headstone has room for fifteen characters per line and four lines total. What would you want it to say and why?

This is one of those questions that make your ethical will not only something that will be cherished by those you love after your death. It is also an opportunity to ask yourself if you are living up to your own ideals. Tell your loved ones what you want your epitaph to say about your life. Then ask yourself if you are living the truth of those words or just pretending. If you don't like the answer, it's never too late to change.

CHAPTER 12

What Will Your Final Blessing Be?

An ending was an ending. No matter how many pages of sentences and paragraphs of great stories led up to it, it would always have the last word.

—Sarah Dessen

The letter came from Hillside Cemetery in June, the kind of letter that always gets my attention: "Buy now, price increase on July 1." I've been to that cemetery five hundred, six hundred times, maybe more. But this time was different. This time it was for me. It was for Betsy. I was buying the last piece of real estate we will ever inhabit.

I look at a few different Leder plot possibilities. Which should it be? Fountain, bench, path, or tree adjacent? "This one," I say to the saleswoman, choosing a double plot between the fountain and the bench. Section 5, row 11, plot 8—my eternal coordinates. I stand on that little rectangle for a good long while. I feel the breeze. It is a strange thing, it is a sobering thing, to stand upon one's own grave.

I imagine the appropriately solemn funeral director in the viewing room prior to the ceremony saying to Betsy, Aaron, and Hannah, "Take your time," as she props open the plain pine casket lid. They lean over to gaze upon my body—waxen and empty of life. Everything feels like it's in slow motion in a surreal gray fog. They see like never before death up close. They feel like never before they too will someday die.

After the viewing I see Betsy bereft, Aaron and his future wife, Hannah and her future husband, their children, my grandchildren, sitting beneath a green awning on white folding chairs. I feel the urge to speak before some other rabbi helps them tear the black ribbon, utter the words, and turn spades of earth upon my casket. Not about myself, but about the people I so deeply love. What, I wonder, should I say in those final moments before they turn from my grave and move slowly back into the world? Mostly, I want to say, "I love you, I love you, I love you," a thousand times and then a thousand times more. I want to hire planes to write enough "I love you's" to fill the sky. There is nothing that matters in the end but love.

I would ask Aaron and Hannah to take care of Betsy and to take care of each other too. I want to remind them that unlike my body, my love for them will never die. I want to hold them and promise them they will eventually be at peace with my death because we shared so much beauty and love in life. I want to wipe their tears and protect them from the pain. "Be good. Be kind," I tell them gently. "Be happy again. Forgive the worst of me, and hold the best of me in your hearts."

But I can't tell them anything. I am gone.

When the funeral ends, they climb back into a dark limousine. Aaron loosens his tie, Hannah and Betsy kick off their shoes, and they journey home to bagels and stories, a flickering candle, and the Mourner's Prayer. They will cry and they will laugh, then cry again.

This final question about imagined last words is predicated on the impossible. None of us will ever get to speak to the people we love who gather at our funeral. If there is a subtext to this entire book, a single lesson amid its many questions and answers, it is simply this: Don't wait. Don't withhold your final blessing until you can no longer bestow it. Don't wait to tell your story.

Remember that you are love and you come from love.
Live for the living, sit with full presence, and speak from your heart.

⌒

Thank you for giving me my reason to live. Be honest. Be true to our faith. Think of me when you read a good novel, see a rainbow, or eat a juicy piece of brisket.

⌒

I had the luckiest life. I had the best family and friends. I would tell them to go find your happiness. Go have fun today, right now, with each other, after this funeral and live every day like it's a gathering after days like this, where you hold each other, eat great food, have deep talks, and the rest of the world disappears. Dance, run, sing, hug, and feel. That's what life is.

⌒

My dear ones,

I love you, I am proud of you, and I believe in you. Although I am not with you in person, may these guidelines of spirit be a lighthouse to help you find your way.

Be kind to yourselves. Be kind to each other. Do your best to nurture the relationships within your family. Find pleasures and joy during your time on this earth and seek ways to leave this

*world a little bit better than you found it. Make meaning
through loving connection and simple things rather
than by chasing power, dominance, fame, or money.
You are enough and you have enough. Reach out and
give back.*

*Show empathy and show you care. Find your people. Be
welcoming and inclusive. Be a fiercely loyal and trustworthy
friend. However, if a group or someone demonstrates they don't
want you, don't value you, or repeatedly betrays you, don't try to
convince them of your worth. That is a them problem. They are
not your people. Temper your anger. Manage the gift of your
disappointment. Walk away. Replant your garden. Vacuum.
Cook something. Be kind.*

*Stare three things straight in the eye: cruelty, dishonesty, and
pain. Don't flinch, don't look away. Confront mean-spiritedness,
including gossip, directly and clearly. Walk toward those in pain
and do whatever you can in a caring way to help and create
change with family, friends, and those less fortunate in our
community and around the world.*

*Find work you enjoy well enough and perform it with
integrity. Dance, sing, and swim with abandon—especially in
foreign waters. Travel to expand your heart and understanding
of others. Listen to live music. Let loose sometimes. Drink good
whiskey or wine. At the same time, watch for addiction and
mental illness, which run in our family. Ask for, get, and accept*

help when needed. Trust in a good night's sleep and the promise
of a new day.

> *All my love,*
> *Mom*

❧

Be kind to each other, take care of each other, and never forget how important your family is to your life.

❧

Please know that a day didn't go by that I wasn't grateful for every one of you. My heart was full each time I saw your face or heard your voice. You have all worried too much about disappointing me—I was always proud of how you are in the world, and the world is made better every day you are in it. Keep the love I had for you someplace where you can draw from it and know that I'm always there with you, cheering you on, believing in you and your dreams.

❧

I would say, Thank you for loving me, accepting me, holding me, supporting me, and caring for me. I would bless them with strength to withstand their pain, wonder to see the beauty of life, joy to experience the holiness of living, and love to greet each day and themselves.

~

Love. Love. Love. Love wins. That's it, that's all. No matter what else happens, try to find a way to love your way through it.

~

Please take care of my wife. I can't be there for her now—so I beg you to grant her comfort and respect and the fullness of your love. Please be blessings to each other. Care for each other, celebrate with each other, stay close to each other. No one will ever love you as I love you because no one will ever know you as I have known you. You have brought meaning and purpose to every one of my days. I am so proud of each of you. You have forgiven me numerous times. I apologize for that. But I did the best that I could. You know most of my failings, but not all. You know most of what I am proud of, but not all.

I didn't want to depart. But I am comfortable leaving my world in your hands. When you see a proud orca cresting the waves, think of me. Your images were the very last images held by my brain and by my heart.

❧

My final blessing would be the Priestly—it is something
I have always found to bring me such enormous peace at
the end of services, my wedding, my children's mitzvahs:

❧

May the Eternal bless you and protect you.

❧

May the Eternal be kind and gracious to you.

❧

May the Eternal bestow favor upon you and grant you peace.

❧

I've had plenty of time to prepare for this final
act. It's your turn now! I remind you to pay attention
to your life as you live it. Stop and assess to see if
you are being your best self and then ask yourself
if you would be proud to know you. All love—that's
all folks!

❧

Appreciate what you have and go deeper. Take
time to really look at the art on our walls and
at the books in our library. Always be learning.
Be interested in others. Everyone has a story

and some of those stories are life-changing. Make new friends. Be in touch with old friends. Take on projects. Help others. Show up. The rest is commentary.

❧

I'm in heaven now, at peace and with God. I will watch over all of you. Go out and shine God's light.

❧

Today I am both sad and happy. I am sad because I don't know when I will see my family and friends again. I already miss everyone so much. I am happy because those closest to me are here paying their final respects to me. You can have wealth, and material things, and success, but nothing beats a great family and friends. Without that, everything else is meaningless.

I had a full life because I was surrounded by great people. I was the lucky one. My childhood may have been without things, but my parents loved me and gave me everything that was really important: love, a great education, and the desire to achieve. I was also surrounded by great friends. I attended great schools and I married an incredible woman and had two terrific children. Yes, I was the lucky one.

Then at fifty-eight, my first real adversity: the illness of a child. I cried, I studied, I sought advice, and ultimately my beautiful boy came through the other side of a hellish illness. My past worries of where I might attend school, or where I would work, or whether I would win a case, were nonsense compared to what I needed but couldn't seem to do for my son. I found out quickly who my true friends were. They wanted to give me comfort and support, but I was so used to helping others, I couldn't let them help me. Let people help you when you are hurting. That is what friends are for. I just couldn't.

My children, I cannot tell you how proud I am of the both of you. I want you to love your family and friends. I want you to give back because of the opportunities you have that others don't. I want you to be kind and good and strive to be mensches.

Your family must come first. A wise lawyer once told me that I would never regret missing a day of work, but I would never forgive myself if I missed my kids' games or events. I never did. Because I refused to miss those moments, I have very few regrets when it comes to having seen you grow up. That lawyer's advice was maybe the best advice I ever got. It would be nice if you took my advice once in a while.

My wife, you were my good person compass. You have a heart of gold and you made me a better person. I was lucky to have you as my wife.

My blessing to all of my loved ones is that you do what you are passionate about and what makes you happy. That you give back and be on the forefront of maintaining our heritage and traditions. I know you will.

I do not plan to wait until the end of my funeral, but will have the conversation when the end is near. They know I love them. Remembering me—any way they wish to do this—need not be and should not be accompanied by sadness, just memories. We do not know what happens to me, but the likelihood is only the peace of painlessness. More important is what happens to my family. I would in blessing ask that they go forward as they alone know how to do.

May their lives be for a blessing. The statement really denotes that life is brief, that there are lives that are not fulfilled, and that there are lives that are of limited consequence. Let theirs not be included among them.

I know that that is a negative explanation of a positive blessing. I guess I'll need a little more time to refine that one.

Your mom and I did our best to bring you up in a home that was secure, one in which there was no sense of danger, real or imagined. We "spared the rod," the recriminations, the hurt, and the threats, and we, in turn, were spared the tumult of a dangerous world. We built this home and this upbringing with the thought in mind that one cannot undo the effects of perceived danger, but the concept of safety in childhood could help you find peace and safety for the rest of your lives, even if things change.

My final blessing would be to encourage my family to feel gratitude, to say yes to life, to be fully present and not to fear the leap into intimacy, vulnerability, real honesty, and deep love. I would wish them the blessing of being real and raw and authentic with every connection and I'd wish them the blessing of extra cheese on their pizzas and extra hot fudge on their sundaes, extra days off to play at the beach. I'd wish them the blessing I so often in my past denied myself—to leap from what's comfortable to find out who you are and how deeply you can love and experience joy.

~

Do not grieve. I am not gone. I am all around you all the time. Go forward, not backward. I'm coming with you.

~

If you could speak to your family at the end of your own funeral, what would you say? What would your final blessing to them be?

This is the last of my questions. I hope you will answer it along with all the others in this book and then use those answers as the raw material to write your own ethical will. Make it a love letter to the people you love most. Let them wrap themselves in your values, your faith, your hard-earned wisdom and steadfast love. Tell them your truth. Tell them your story so they hold you in their hearts as you have held them in yours; now, and when you are gone.

Epilogue

A word is dead
When it is said,
Some say.
I say it just
Begins to live
That day.

—Emily Dickinson

Mostly, writing is hard work, emotional torture even. Whoever first said, "Writing is easy; you just open a vein and bleed," nailed it. I sometimes stare at the computer screen for hours. Many times the best I can do is write with the same feeling I had when I shoveled snow off the driveway of my Minnesota childhood home—push, lift, throw, push, lift, throw, row, after row, after row. It is dull, exhausting grunt work, and a little depressing because you know it's going to snow again tomorrow when the editor sends notes, and you're going to have to shovel the same damn driveway all over again.

But then, there are those rare, perfect, timeless moments when the words come through me, not from me; as if my fingers are a conduit for inspiration from the heavens for which I am merely an earthly messenger. It is magic and more than enough to make it worth the journey through writing hell to get there.

I have felt that miraculous flow both times I sat down to write an ethical will to my children. Each literally took only minutes for me to craft and needed almost no editing at all. When I ask myself why, I think the reason is related to that quote about writing being like opening a vein except that it was my heart, not a vein, that was opened. And no doubt it is also because, as I said at the beginning, I have been asking the questions in this book for years, of others and of myself. As promised in the beginning of our journey together through the questions that tell our life story, here is my ethical will, my truth, my bequest to the ones I love most, for now and for when I am gone.

Dear Aaron and Hannah,

The finest moments of my life have been with you and Mommy, sitting around our kitchen table, laughing. I never feel richer or more at peace with the world than in those moments. That kind of love is more important than anything. Spend your life with a person as good as Mommy and you will have many of those moments. And don't worry, you will know in your heart when that person arrives. It is a powerful, healing, beautiful kind of love. Grasp it.

Have a healthy relationship with work. Do your best at it, but your work is not the same thing as your life. I often confused the two and hope you will less so. Spend time in nature. It will remind you of God, of true greatness; it will calm you, cause you to pause, breathe, stand still, listen. It will help you feel humble and small in profound and important ways. Think of me when you are out there; feel and know that my soul is with you.

Do not roll your eyes at religion. Celebrate what makes you different. There is much to learn—much—from our ancestors, from prayer, the Sabbath, candles, warm bread and wine, generosity, and faith while gathered around a table with people you love—much.

When you worry, remember that most things turn out better than we expect. When anxiety, sorrow, loss, and pain come, lean on the people you love. Do not suffer alone; it is much worse that way. This is another reason you should look for someone like Mommy to love. I would not have been able to breathe without her.

I used to love to dance, but when I became a more public person, I stopped dancing at weddings and parties. I allowed my fear of what others might think of me, fear of being a spectacle, to keep me from dancing. I regret that now. It was a bad example to you and robbed me of joy. Don't let fear of what others might think keep you from dancing or singing or loving. Let nothing and no one suppress what your soul longs for. Live so that you do not die with a longing soul.

Count your blessings. When you are feeling less than, or want more, or are mired in self-pity, which happens to us all, look around and count your blessings again and again and again until you tally a hundred of them. Everything is easier when you are grateful.

Feel for others. People behave badly because they are damaged. Let your first impulse be one of empathy. That being said, there will be a handful of people in your life who demand too much—who are mean, narcissistic, negative—causing you to feel terrible about yourself. Cut these people out of your life. You cannot fix them.

Be good and the rest works out. See the world with the people you love. Cherish time; it matters so much more than things. Mine with you and Mommy has made my life worth living. I wish for you that kind of love now. I wish for you that kind of love when I am gone. Say the Mourner's Prayer and light a candle for me when I am gone. Feel its warmth and know I love you still.

Dad

Let me make you a promise. If you follow the example of those who honestly addressed each question in this book, you will have the raw material you need to write your own ethical will. Most of the people who contributed answers, it's worth noting, do not consider themselves "writers," and some of them were thinking about some of these questions for the first time. I promise if you sincerely consider these questions and if when you sit down to write your ethical will your heart is fully open, that magical flow will be yours and it will take you only minutes, not hours or days, to complete. When you are done, share it with the people you wrote it for, the people you love. Give them their own copy to keep. It will surely be among the most valuable of treasures for them to hold when you are gone.

Acknowledgments

While I promised them anonymity and therefore cannot mention them by name, my deepest gratitude to each of my friends—the scholars, political and religious leaders, writers, journalists, celebrities, teachers, and fellow observers of life who graciously agreed to answer the twelve challenging questions that are the heartbeat of this book. I am deeply grateful also to the finest team any writer could hope for: my agent and confidante, Stephanie Tade; gifted editors Caroline Sutton and Stephanie Higgs, as well as Caroline's assistants Hannah Steigmeyer and Natasha Soto; PR gurus Anne Kosmoski, Farin Schlussel, and Mara Freedman; and copyeditor Kim Lewis. Thank you to Gretchen van Nuys for securing the necessary permissions for material quoted in the manuscript and to my assistant, Samantha Rosen, for managing so many details of my life and work.

This book is for the people who matter most to each of us. With total sincerity I want you, the reader, to know that you matter to me. This book is for you and your loved ones. It is from my heart to yours. Since my own father's death, I have